KU-470-145

SAUERKRAUT'S
Incredible FASCINATIONS

Shirley Hensley

Trafford
PUBLISHING™

Order this book online at www.trafford.com/07-3013
or email orders@trafford.com

Most Trafford titles are also available at major online book retailers.

© Copyright 2008 Shirley Hensley
All rights reserved. No part of this publication may be reproduced, stored in a retrieval
system, or transmitted, in any form or by any means, electronic, mechanical, photocopying,
recording, or otherwise, without the written prior permission of the author.

Note for Librarians: A cataloguing record for this book is available from Library
and Archives Canada at www.collectionscanada.ca/amicus/index-e.html

ISBN: 978-1-4251-6520-8

*We at Trafford believe that it is the responsibility of us all, as both individuals
and corporations, to make choices that are environmentally and socially sound.
You, in turn, are supporting this responsible conduct each time you purchase a
Trafford book, or make use of our publishing services. To find out how you are
helping, please visit www.trafford.com/responsiblepublishing.html*

*Our mission is to efficiently provide the world's finest, most comprehensive
book publishing service, enabling every author to experience success.
To find out how to publish your book, your way, and have it available
worldwide, visit us online at www.trafford.com/10510*

 www.trafford.com

North America & international
toll-free: 1 888 232 4444 (USA & Canada)
phone: 250 383 6864 ♦ fax: 250 383 6804 ♦ email: info@trafford.com

The United Kingdom & Europe
phone: +44 (0)1865 722 113 ♦ local rate: 0845 230 9601
facsimile: +44 (0)1865 722 868 ♦ email: info.uk@trafford.com

10 9 8 7 6 5 4 3

I chose to include a color picture of only one of the recipes on the front cover of this book. There are no other pictures of any of the other recipes. This will save on the printing costs of this book and pass the savings on to you when you purchase it. You can still enjoy all the sauerkraut recipes and save money too. After all, we all want more for our dough, right?

Table of Contents

SAUERKRAUT'S
Incredible FASCINATIONS

Astonishingly impressive Sauerkraut recipes
with an astounding taste!!!

Introduction

I HAVE VERY vivid childhood memories involving sauerkraut. Many times I watched my mother bring in the cabbage, clean it up, chop it up and can it as sauerkraut. (My canning and freezing recipes for sauerkraut are in the book).

Being raised in the South, we would have some tremendous storms that would knock out our electricity many times. During the hours of darkness, my mother's method of keeping me calm was, "Where were you when the lights went out? Down in the cellar eating sauerkraut!" Eventually, all she would do whenever the electricity went out was ask the question; my reply would be, "Down in the cellar eating sauerkraut!" I thank God for giving me a mother who fed me lots of sauerkraut all during my growing years into adulthood.

About the Author

SHIRLEY HENSLEY WAS born and raised in Louisville, Kentucky. However, half of her relatives on her father's side reside in Tennessee. She spent much of her growing up years in Tennessee. How could she ever forget walking with her grandmother and help her carry buckets of water from the flowing spring on her property, then drinking it out of a dipper? At night, her grandma's lighting was coal-oil lamps. Shirley remembers too, sleeping on "grandma's feather bed and feather pillows."

Shirley's favorite memory was watching her grandmother and aunts make homemade sauerkraut. "I always enjoyed watching my relatives make home-made sauerkraut. More than that, I love getting a big tablespoon and eat it right out of the jar after it was ready. Even today, when I visit my aunt, she would open a jar of sauerkraut, give me a tablespoon, and I would gobble it down. Needless to say, she would love watching me enjoy myself." As you probably now know, sauerkraut is one of Shirley's favorite foods. Shirley keeps a jar of sauerkraut in her refrigerator and snacks on it once a day.

Down home cooking and traveling are Shirley's two favorite activities. As a result of her love of cooking and traveling various parts of the world, she has collected hundreds of recipes from many people and places, and within her family tree.

She loves sharing with people worldwide all the blessings that have been granted to her during her lifetime, her favorite being, cooking with sauerkraut.

How to Make Sauerkraut

~ 25 pounds cabbage
~ ¾ cup pickling salt
~ (Be sure to use non-iodized because iodine will prevent the bacterial fermentation necessary to change cabbage into sauerkraut)

Work with about 5 pounds of cabbage at a time. (For best sauerkraut, use firm heads of fresh cabbage. Shred cabbage and start kraut between 24 and 48 hours after harvest). Discard outer leaves. Rinse heads under cold running water and drain. Cut heads in quarters and remove cores. Shred or slice to a thickness of a quarter. Put cabbage in wood crock or suitable fermentation container. Add 3 tablespoons of salt. Mix thoroughly using clean hands. Pack firmly until salt draws juices from cabbage. Repeat shredding, slating and packing until all cabbage is in the container. Be sure it is deep enough so that its rim is at least 4-5 inches above the cabbage. If juice does not cover the cabbage, add boiled and cooled brine (1½ tablespoons salt per quart of water). Add plates and weights; cover container with a clean cheesecloth. Store at 70-75 degrees Fahrenheit while fermenting. At temperatures between 70-75 degrees F, kraut will be fully fermented in about 3-4 weeks; at temperatures lower than 60 degrees F, kraut may not ferment. Above 75 degrees F, kraut may become soft. If you weigh the cabbage down with a brine-filled bag, do not disturb the crock until normal fermentation is completed (when bubbling ceases). If you use jars as weight, you will have to check the kraut 2-3 times each week and remove scum, if it forms – it is not harmful, but it can affect the flavor. After kraut's fermented, rinse in cold water. It is now ready to use. Fully fermented kraut may be kept tightly covered in the refrigerator for several months, or it may be canned for future use.

Canning Sauerkraut

HOT PACK METHOD:

Bring kraut and liquid slowly to a boil in a large kettle, stirring frequently. Remove from heat and fill jars rather firmly with kraut and juices, leaving ½ inch headspace. Adjust lids. Process pints 10 minutes and quarts 15 minutes in the boiling water canner.

RAW (COLD) PACK METHOD:

Fill jars firmly with kraut and cover with juices, leaving ½ inch headspace. Adjust lids. Process pints 20 minutes and quarts 25 minutes in the boiling water canner.

Odorless Sauerkraut in Jars

CUT CABBAGE AS for slaw. Salt it and put it in a stone jar, sprinkling salt on it, then pressing it down until packed. Let it ferment for about 1 week. Put it on the stove in a cooking vessel and let it boil in its own brine for a few minutes. Have sterilized jars ready. Fill the jars with kraut, stuffing well, and seal them tight. When sauerkraut is done in this manner, it will keep for years and be odorless.

Freezing Sauerkraut

AFTER FERMENTATION, REMOVE and pack sauerkraut and juice in rigid plastic moisture or vapour-proof freezer containers, or in glass freezer jars (leaving 1½ inch headspace), or in heavy tightly-sealed plastic freezer bags. Freeze.

Breads

Breadmaker Reuben Bread

~ 2 ½ tsp active yeast
~ 2 ¼ cup bread flour
~ 1 cup rye flour
~ 2 tbsp gluten
~ 1 tsp salt
~ ½ tsp dry mustard
~ ⅛ tsp baking soda
~ 1 tsp caraway seeds
~ 3 ounce Swiss cheese, shredded
~ ¼ cup sauerkraut, rinsed and drained
~ 3 tbsp Thousand Island dressing
~ 1 cup plus 2 tbsp warm water
~ 2 ½ ounce deli-sliced, lean corned beef

All ingredients must be at room temperature, except water which should be 110 degrees F. Add all ingredients to breadmaker in the order listed. Select white bread and start buttons. Great taste as toast or in a sandwich.

Sauerkraut Onion Bread

~ 2 ¼ cup bread flour
~ 1 cup milk
~ ¾ tsp salt
~ ¼ tsp onion salt
~ 2 tbsp butter
~ ½ cup sauerkraut, drained, rinsed and finely chopped
~ 1 tbsp onion, finely chopped
~ ½ cup whole wheat flour
~ ¾ cup rye flour
~ 1 ½ tbsp white sugar
~ ½ tbsp caraway seed
~ 1 ¾ tsp active dry yeast

Add all the ingredients to the bread pan in the order listed. Place the bread pan in the bread machine and close the lid. Select the basic setting and press start.

Simply Sauerkraut Bread

~ 1 (1/4 oz) pkg dry yeast
~ ¾ cup warm water
~ ½ cup potato flakes
~ 3 tbsp packed brown sugar
~ 1 tsp salt
~ ½ tsp caraway seed
~ 2 tbsp vegetable oil
~ 1 (14 oz) can sauerkraut, drained and chopped
~ 3 ½ - 4 cups flour

In a large bowl, sprinkle yeast over water. Stir until dissolved. Blend in potato flakes, brown sugar, salt, caraway seed, oil and sauerkraut. Gradually add flour to make stiff dough. Knead on floured surface for 4 minutes. Cover and let rinse in warm spot until doubled in size, about 45 minutes to 1 hour. Preheat oven to 350 degrees. Bake for 50-60 minutes or until deep golden brown.

Sauerkraut Rye Bread

~   3 cups whole rye flour
~   1 envelope dry yeast
~   2 cups warm water
~   1 ½ cups sauerkraut, undrained
~   2 tbsp vegetable shortening
~   1 ½ tbsp caraway seeds
~   2 tsp salt
~   4 ½ cups unbleached flour
~   1 egg white

Start sponge 6–18 hours before you plan to make bread. In a large bowl, mix 2 cups of the rye flour, yeast, and 1 ½ cups of water until smooth. Cover with plastic wrap and let stand at room temperature for at least 6 but no longer than 18 hours. (The mixture rises and falls as it ferments but should appear as a soft dough mass when ready).

Add sauerkraut, remaining ½ cup warm water, shortening, caraway seeds, salt, and remaining cup of rye flour; mix well with wooden spoon. Gradually, stir in 3 cups of the unbleached flour to make a stiff dough. (The dough will be quite sticky at first, becoming smoother and more elastic as flour is added in the next steps). Turn dough onto floured surface and knead for 10 minutes, adding enough of the remaining flour to keep dough from sticking. Knead until smooth, elastic, and no longer sticky. Place dough in large clean bowl. Cover and let rise in a warm place until almost tripled in volume (1 ½ - 2 hours). Punch dough down; divide in half, knead each piece a few times, then shape into smooth round or oval loaves. Place each loaf on a greased cookie sheet. Cover loosely with a towel and let rise until almost double in volume (about 50 minutes). Preheat oven to 400 degrees. Brush tops and sides of loaves with the beaten egg white. Make 3-4 slashes, ½ inch deep, on surface of loaves with a very sharp knife. Bake on middle rack in oven for 35 to 40 minutes or until crust is golden brown and loaves sound hollow when tapped. Slide onto cooling rack. Can be served slightly warm or completely cooled. Makes 2 loaves.

Cottage Cheese Kraut Bread

~ 1 tbsp dry yeast
~ ¼ cup warm water
~ ½ cup cottage cheese
~ 2 tbsp brown sugar
~ 1 tbsp margarine
~ 1 tsp salt
~ 1 egg
~ 2 tsp caraway seeds
~ 2 tsp minced onion
~ 2 ¼ cup flour
~ 1 cup sauerkraut

In a bowl, dissolve yeast in warm water. In a saucepan, combine cottage cheese and salt; heat to lukewarm (100 degrees). Add yeast to cottage cheese mixture. Stir in egg, caraway seeds, onion, and ¼ cup of flour. Beat this batter very well. Add rest of flour thoroughly. Stir in sauerkraut. Turn mixture onto floured surface and knead until plump. Put in greased bowl; cover and leave in warm place until doubled in size, about 1 ½ hours. Punch down and put in greased bread pan. Let rise again until doubled in size. Preheat oven to 400 degrees. Bake 20-25 minutes. Bread is done when crust gives a hollow sound when tapped.

Sandwiches

Reuben Sandwich

~ 2 tbsp Thousand Island dressing
~ ¼ cup chilled sauerkraut, well drained
~ 2 slices dark rye bread
~ 2 tsp soft butter
~ 4 slices Swiss cheese
~ 4 slices Kosher style corned beef
~ 1 tbsp mustard

Mix Thousand Island dressing with sauerkraut. Spread outside of bread slices with soft butter. Place bread, buttered side down, side by side on a plate. Place Swiss cheese on each slice of bread; place corned beef on only one slice; add some kraut dressing on the corned beef. Assemble the sandwich to be grilled on a sandwich grill or skillet. If skillet is used, press down with a spatula until sandwich is browned on both sides and cheese oozes. Remove from skillet. When cool enough to touch, lift top slice of bread; add one tablespoon mustard or to taste. Reapply bread. Serve immediately. Serves 2.

Variations: You may substitute pastrami, or turkey, in place of corned beef, for a change.

Chicken Reuben Sandwich

~ Baked chicken breast halves, boneless
~ 8 slices rye bread
~ 4 ounces slices Swiss cheese
~ 1 pound (jar or pkg) sauerkraut, drained, squeezed dry, not rinsed
~ ⅓ cup light mayonnaise
~ 2 tbsp ketchup

Turn on broiler, with rack 4 inches from the heat. Thinly slice chicken. Top 4 slices of bread with cheese, then with chicken and sauerkraut. In small bowl, stir together mayonnaise and ketchup; spoon over sauerkraut. Place remaining slices of bread over top. Broil sandwiches about 2 minutes on each side, until cheese has melted and bread is golden brown. Cut in half and serve immediately. Serves 4.

German-Style Bratwurst and Kraut

~ 16 Bratwurst links
~ 16 Bratwurst buns
~ 2 tbsp butter
~ 2 cups onion, chopped
~ 2 cloves garlic, chopped
~ 2 pounds sauerkraut, drained
~ 2 tsp chicken stock powder
~ 1 tsp caraway seed
~ 1 bay leaf
~ 1 cup chopped apples (1/4 inch cubes)

Melt butter in a 4 quart pot over medium high heat. Add onion and garlic and sauté until tender. Add sauerkraut, chicken stock powder, caraway seeds, and bay leaf. Reduce heat and simmer on low heat uncovered for 5 minutes. Stir in chopped apples and simmer an additional 5-10 minutes. Remove bay leaf and cover pot to stay warm. Set sauerkraut aside. Grill bratwurst as directed on package. Place bratwurst in buns and top with sauerkraut. Serves 16.

Layered Sauerkraut Veggie Sandwich
(see next page for layering instructions)

~ Bread
~ Butter

(a)
~ radishes, sliced
~ cucumber, sliced
~ sour cream
~ parsley, chopped

(b)
~ tomatoes, sliced
~ hard cooked eggs, sliced
~ chives, chopped

(c)
~ horseradish
~ salt and pepper

(d)
~ romaine lettuce, chopped
~ spinach, chopped
~ onions, sliced in strips
~ green pepper, sliced in strips

(e)
~ sauerkraut
~ grated cheese

(f)
~ olive oil
~ ranch dressing
~ red wine vinaigrette

Spread bread slices generously with butter and top with the following in order:

(a) sliced radishes and cucumbers dipped in sour cream and sprinkled with parsley

(b) sliced tomatoes and hard cooked eggs garnished with chives

(c) season with horseradish and salt and pepper

(d) add chopped lettuce, chopped spinach; cover with strips of onions and green pepper

(e) top with sauerkraut and grated cheese (any type of grated cheese)

(f) add olive oil, ranch dressing, and red wine vinaigrette to taste

Tip: can use slices of whole grain, oat nut, rye or pumpernickel bread. If you prefer white bread, French bread, or Italian bread, that's fine too.

Caraway Sauerkraut and Split Frank Sandwiches

~ 6 frankfurters
~ 1 tbsp caraway seeds
~ 2 cups sauerkraut, drained, reserve juice
~ 12 slices thin rye bread
~ 3 tbsp Dijonnaise (or equal mixture of mustard and mayonnaise)

Cut frankfurters lengthwise without cutting all the way through. In a non-stick skillet, over medium heat, lay hotdogs flat; fry 2 minutes on each side. Remove to a platter and keep warm; keep heat under pan. Add caraway seeds to pan and toast 30 seconds; add sauerkraut. Add small amounts of sauerkraut juice if mixture begins to stick to pan. Meantime, toast bread and spread equal amount of mustard/mayonnaise (Dijonnaise) on each slice. Place franks on each of six slices of bread. Top each with even amounts of sauerkraut mixture, and top with remaining bread slices.

Tip: the split franks can be spread out in an oven-proof casserole dish, covered with kraut mixture and cooked in a 375 degree oven for 20 minutes. Five minutes before serving, arrange bread on cookie sheets and toast in oven. Serves 6.

Red Sauerkraut and Frankfurters

~ 2 cups sauerkraut, drained
~ ½ cup condensed tomato soup
~ 1 tsp cayenne pepper
~ 6 frankfurters
~ 6 frankfurter buns

Heat oven to 375 degrees. Combine the sauerkraut, soup, and cayenne pepper in an oven-proof dish; stir to mix well. Press frankfurters into the kraut mixture over the frankfurters. Bake for 20 minutes or until mixture begins to bubble. Two minutes before serving, open buns and put on oven rack to heat through. Transfer a hotdog to each bun and mound kraut mixture on top. Serves 6.

Confetti Kraut and Frankfurters

~ ½ medium onion, chopped
~ 1 tbsp butter
~ 2 cups (16 oz) sauerkraut, drained
~ ⅓ cup raisins
~ ¼ cup grated carrot
~ ½ cup apple juice
~ 8 frankfurters
~ 8 frankfurter buns

In a medium saucepan, sauté onion in butter until soft. Mix in sauerkraut, raisins, carrot, and apple juice. Bring to a boil; cover and simmer 15 minutes. Meanwhile, in medium saucepan, cover frankfurters with water and simmer 10 minutes or until heated through; drain. Place frankfurters in buns and top with sauerkraut mixture. Serves 8.

Sweet and Hot Piccalilli Dogs

~ 1 pound bratwurst or frankfurters
~ 1 pkg hotdog buns
~ 1 cup sauerkraut, drained with juice reserved
~ ½ cup mild sweet pickle relish
~ 3 tbsp onion, chopped
~ ¼ tsp celery seeds
~ 1 tsp caraway seeds

Grill bratwurst or frankfurters until done. In a small bowl, combine the drained sauerkraut, sweet pickle relish, and onion. In a small saucepan, combine the reserved kraut juice, celery seeds, and caraway seeds. Heat to boiling and simmer for 2-3 minutes. Pour over the kraut mixture and toss. Set aside to cool, then transfer to covered container and store in the refrigerator, until ready to use. Bring to room temperature and serve over bratwursts or frankfurters in a hotdog bun.

Thousand Island Bacon Dogs

~   ½ cup Thousand Island dressing
~   1 ½ cups sauerkraut, drained
~   1 pkg all-beef franks
~   1 pkg hotdog buns
~   bacon, fried and crumbled

In skillet, fry bacon until crisp. Drain on paper towel. Mix well, the Thousand Island dressing into the sauerkraut. Set aside. Meanwhile, in medium saucepan, cover hotdogs with water and simmer 10 minutes or until heated through; drain. (If you prefer to broil your hotdogs, place hotdogs on baking pan in a preheated 350 degree oven for 10-15 minutes or until browned). Place hotdogs on hotdog buns. Speak sauerkraut mixture over them. Sprinkle each hotdog with crumbled bacon to taste.

Crunchy Onion Dogs

~ 1 ½ cups sauerkraut, drained
~ 1 can (6 oz) French onion rings
~ 1 pkg all-beef franks
~ 1 pkg hotdog buns

In medium saucepan, cover hotdogs with water and simmer 10 minutes or until heated through; drain. Place hotdogs on hotdog buns. Spread sauerkraut, (drained), over them. Top with coarsely chopped French onion rings to taste instead of chopped onion.

Cream Cheese Kraut Dogs

~ ¼ cup butter
~ 1 Walla Walla onion, thinly sliced
~ 1 (4 oz) pkg cream cheese
~ 4 hotdogs or your favorite sausages
~ 4 hotdog buns
~ brown mustard
~ sauerkraut

Preheat grill or grill pan to medium high heat. Melt butter in a skillet over medium heat. Add onions and cook slowly until the onions have softened and turned deep brown, about 15 minutes. Microwave cream cheese for 15-30 seconds until very soft. Grill hotdogs until well browned. Lightly grill hotdog buns on both sides. To assemble cheese dogs, spread warm cream cheese on toasted hotdog bun, add hotdog or sausage, top with onions, mustard, and sauerkraut.

Kraut Swiss Round Dogs

~ 2 cups sauerkraut, undrained
~ 1 tsp basil leaves
~ 8 hamburger buns, split
~ 8 slices Swiss cheese
~ 8 frankfurters

Combine sauerkraut and basil in saucepan. Cover and cook over low heat, stirring occasionally for 10 minutes; drain. Top bun halves with cheese slices and broil 5-7 inches from source of heat 3-5 minutes or until browned. Cut 10 deep slits into each frankfurter without cutting all the way through. Broil 5-7 inches from source of heat 3-5 minutes. Turn and broil 3 minutes longer. Place frankfurters on bun bottoms; top with sauerkraut mixture and bun tops. Serves 8.

Mexican Kraut Round Dogs

~ 1 medium onion, chopped
~ 4 cups sauerkraut, drained
~ 1 (10 ¼ oz) can marinara sauce
~ 8 corn tortillas
~ 8 green pepper rings
~ 8 frankfurters
~ 1 (8 oz) can whole kernel corn, heated and drained

Sauté onion in vegetable oil until golden. Add kraut and marinara sauce; mix well. Cover and cook over low heat for 30 minutes. Fry tortillas in 1 inch vegetable oil until crisp; drain on paper towels. Fry green pepper rings 1 minute and drain. Cut 7-10 parallel slits in each frankfurter without cutting all the way through. Broil 5-7 inches from source of heat or cook on outdoor grill 3-5 minutes. Turn and broil 3 minutes. Top each tortilla with kraut, round dog, then green pepper ring. Fill center of round dog with corn. Makes 8 sandwiches.

Smoked Turkey Krautwich on Bun

~ 4 tbsp mayonnaise
~ 4 tbsp hamburger pickle relish
~ 8 slices rye bread
~ 1 pound smoked turkey breast
~ 1 jar (4 ounces) roasted red peppers
~ 2 cups sauerkraut, undrained
~ 4 slices Swiss cheese
~ 4 Kosher dill pickles

Preheat oven to 400 degrees. Combine mayonnaise and relish. Spread on each slice of bread, dividing evenly. Divide turkey and place on top of four slices of bread. Cut peppers into strips and mix with sauerkraut; place equal amount of sauerkraut mixture on top of turkey. Add a slice of cheese. Heat in oven until cheese melts, about 3-5 minutes. Remove from oven; top with second slice of bread and serve each sandwich with a pickle. Serves 4.

Tip: These sandwiches can be served "open face."

Soups

Finnish Sauerkraut Soup

~ 12 cups water
~ 1 pound lean pork, cubed
~ 1 ham bone
~ 4 cups sauerkraut, undrained
~ 9 whole allspice
~ Salt and pepper to taste

Combine the water, pork, ham bone, sauerkraut and allspice in a soup kettle. Simmer 2-3 hours or until pork is tender. Add salt and pepper to taste.

Serve as a main course on a cold night accompanied by rye bread, cheese and cold cuts. Serves 10-12.

Meatball and Sauerkraut Soup

~ 1 ½ pound hamburger
~ 1 egg, slightly beaten
~ ½ cup soft bread crumbs
~ 1 ¼ tsp salt
~ 2 tbsp chopped parsley
~ 2 tbsp butter
~ 1 can (10 ½ oz) condensed beef broth, undiluted
~ 1 can (14 oz) sauerkraut, undrained
~ 1 quart tomatoes
~ 1 envelope dry onion soup mix
~ 1 cup sliced carrots
~ 1 cup chopped celery
~ 1 tsp salt

Combine hamburger, egg, bread crumbs, ¼ teaspoon salt, and parsley to form into balls. Brown in the butter in large kettle. When browned, remove balls and set aside. In same kettle, combine the broth, sauerkraut, tomatoes, soup mix, carrots, celery, and 1 tsp salt. Bring to a boil. Simmer, covered, for 30 minutes, stirring occasionally. Add meatballs and simmer 20 minutes longer until vegetables are done.

Potato Sauerkraut Soup

~ 4 cups chicken broth
~ 1 can (10 ¾ oz) cream of mushroom soup
~ 2 tsp dill week
~ 1 (16 oz) can sauerkraut, drained and rinsed
~ 2 tbsp apple cider vinegar
~ 1 medium potato, cut in small pieces
~ 1 medium onion, cut in small pieces
~ 2 medium carrots, cut in small pieces
~ 2 stalks celery, chopped
~ ¾ pounds smoked sausage, cubed

Mix all ingredients together. Cook until vegetables and sausage are done.

Sauerkraut Split Pea Soup

~ 1 (16 oz) pkg dried split peas
~ 2 large jars sauerkraut (32 oz – not Bavarian style)
~ 2 cups onions, chopped
~ 2 tbsp butter
~ salt and pepper to taste

Pour split peas in large bowl; cover with water plus 1 inch; cover bowl with towel or plastic wrap; let sit overnight to soften. Rinse split peas in colander and place in large heavy pot; cover with water. Cover with lid and bring to a boil; then simmering until peas soften. Mash slightly with potato masher if needed. In a large frying pan, melt butter over medium heat. Add chopped onion, sautéing until transparent. Add drained, rinsed sauerkraut. Cook until heated through. Add sauerkraut mixture to peas, stirring well. Add salt and pepper to taste. Let simmer on low heat for about 1 hour. Serve in soup bowls.

Sauerkraut Stew

~ 3 pounds sauerkraut
~ 2 pounds pork roast or pork ribs
~ 2 bay leaves
~ 1 ounce dried mushrooms, chopped
~ 20 black peppercorns
~ 10 allspice berries
~ salt to taste
~ 12 cups beef stock, divided
~ 2 pounds cabbage, chopped
~ 2 tbsp butter
~ 1 pound polish sausage, cut into ½ inch pieces
~ 1 pound slab bacon, cut into ½ inch pieces

Rinse sauerkraut with cold water and drain well. In a large stock pot, combine sauerkraut, pork roast or ribs, bay leaves, mushrooms, peppercorns, allspice, and salt. Add 6 cups beef stock and simmer over low heat for 1-2 hours, or until meat is tender. Remove meat and allow to cool. Place the cabbage in a large saucepan and add remaining 6 cups of beef stock. Bring to a boil and cook uncovered over moderate heat 1 hour, until the cabbage is tender. Add the cabbage and its cooking liquid to the sauerkraut mixture. Remove any bones from the cooked meat and cut into ½ inch cubes. Melt butter in a large skillet; add the cooked meat and smoked sausage. Sauté over medium heat 10 minutes or until browned; add to sauerkraut mixture. In the same skillet, sauté the bacon over medium heat until crisp; drain on paper towels. Add to the sauerkraut mixture. Cover and simmer 1 hour or longer. Makes 12-14 servings.

Sauerkraut Christmas Soup

- ~ 1 pound mushrooms
- ~ ½ pound sauerkraut
- ~ 2 tbsp onions, chopped fine
- ~ 1 quart milk
- ~ 1 tbsp butter
- ~ 2 tbsp shortening
- ~ 2 tbsp flour
- ~ paprika (to garnish)

Wash mushrooms well and cut up small. Cook in 2 quarts of water for ½ hour; then add sauerkraut and cook for another 15 minutes. Melt in saucepan shortening and flour; brown lightly and stir constantly while you pour in your milk; cook until smooth. Add to the mushrooms and sauerkraut. Fry onions in the tablespoon of butter; when lightly browned, pour into soup. Cool altogether for a minute and salt to taste. Sprinkle paprika over all. Serves 6.

Russian Green Bean and Potato Soup

~ 1 tbsp vegetable oil
~ 1 large onion, halved and thinly sliced
~ 4 red potatoes, cubed
~ ½ pound green beans, cut into 1 inch pieces
~ 5 cups vegetables, chicken, or beef broth
~ 2 tbsp whole wheat flour
~ ½ cup sour cream
~ ¾ cup sauerkraut with juice
~ 1 tbsp chopped fresh dill
~ salt and pepper to taste

Heat vegetable oil in a large saucepan over medium heat. Stir in the onion, and gently cook until softened and translucent, about 5 minutes. Add the potatoes and green beans. Cook until the green beans have slightly softened – about 5 more minutes. Add the vegetable stock. Bring to a boil over high heat, then lower the heat to medium-low, cover, and cook until the potatoes have softened – about 15 minutes. Stir the flour into the sour cream. Add flour mixture to simmering soup 1 spoonful at a time. Stir in the sauerkraut and dill. Season to taste with salt and pepper. Simmer for 5 minutes more before serving.

Vegetable Soup with Sauerkraut and Smoked Turkey Breast

~ 3 tbsp butter
~ 1 large onion, chopped
~ 1 large leek, chopped
~ 2 medium carrots, chopped
~ 1 medium celery rib, chopped
~ 1 cup sauerkraut
~ 1 bay leaf
~ ¼ tsp black pepper
~ 1 large baking potato, chopped
~ 3 cups beef broth
~ 2 ½ cups chicken broth
~ 1 extra large egg yolk
~ ½ cup sour cream
~ ½ pound sliced turkey
~ 2 tbsp parsley

Melt the butter. Sauté the onion, leek, carrots, celery, and bay leaf till golden. Add potato, sauerkraut, and broths; simmer for 30 minutes. In a heat proof bowl, blend the egg yolk with sour cream. Add a cup of the hot soup mixture into the bowl and blend. Then add that back to the soup. Do Not Boil, the sour cream will curdle. Add black pepper. Cook another 3 minutes or until heated through. Add the parsley and cool 2 minutes longer. Serve.

Sauerkraut Pickle Soup

~ 1 tbsp olive oil
~ 1 onion, finely diced
~ 1 cup sauerkraut, chopped
~ 1 cup dill pickles, shredded
~ 4 cups chicken broth (low sodium)
~ 1 ham hock
~ salt and pepper to taste

Heat the olive oil in a soup pot. Add the onion and cook until soft, about 5 minutes. Add the sauerkraut, pickles, broth, and ham hock. Cover; bring to a boil; reduce heat to low and simmer for 45 minutes. Season to taste with salt and pepper. Remove ham hock and serve. This soup is delicious when accompanied by sour cream and some fresh dill.

Surprise Chili

- ~ 1 tbsp olive oil
- ~ 1 pound ground beef
- ~ 1 ½ cups chopped onion
- ~ 2 cloves garlic
- ~ 1 can (28 oz) crushed tomatoes
- ~ 1 can sauerkraut (15 oz), rinsed
- ~ 1 jar or can (15 oz) pinto beans
- ~ 1 can (14 oz) beef broth (low sodium)
- ~ 3-4 tbsp chilli powder
- ~ ¼ tsp pepper

Heat oil in 3 quart saucepan. Brown meat, onions, and garlic. Drain. Stir in remaining ingredients. Bring to a boil. Reduce heat to low. Simmer, partially covered for 25-30 minutes. 4-6 servings.

Note: Rinsing sauerkraut prior to draining, removes about ½ of its sodium.

Slovak Soup

~ 6 cups water
~ 1 can (16 oz) sauerkraut, drained, rinsed, cut-up
~ 1 cup cooked mushrooms, chopped
~ 1 can (16 oz) tomatoes, cut up
~ 1 can (16 oz) lima beans or butter beans, drained
~ salt and pepper to taste

Cook sauerkraut in water for 30 minutes. Add mushrooms and tomatoes, cook 15 minutes. Add beans and cook 10 minutes. In skillet, make gravy by adding 1 tbsp flour to 2 tbsp of oil. Cook on low heat until browned. Add 1 cup of cold water and keep stirring until smooth. Pour gravy into soup and cook for 10 more minutes. Add salt and pepper to taste.

Sauerkraut Chowder

~ 3-4 large russet potatoes
~ 1 medium onion, chopped
~ 1 (15 oz) can sauerkraut
~ 1 (10 oz) can evaporated milk
~ 1 (16 oz) pkg Kielbasa, diced
~ 1 (8 oz) pkg cream cheese, softened
~ water
~ salt and pepper to taste

Cut potatoes into bite-sized pieces; place in Dutch oven or soup pot; cover with water. Add onions and boil until potatoes are done and fork tender. When potatoes ore done, add sauerkraut, evaporated milk, and cream cheese; stir until cream cheese is completely blended. At this time, add the Kielbasa. Add salt and pepper to taste. Cover and cook on low heat; simmer for 30 minutes.

Reuben Soup

~ 6-8 slices rye bread, toasted and quartered
~ 1 ½ tbsp butter
~ ½ cup onion, finely chopped
~ ¼ cup celery, finely chopped
~ 1 ½ (16 oz) cans chicken broth, (24 oz total)
~ ¼ cup quick cooking tapioca
~ 1 cup sauerkraut, well drained
~ ½ pound deli-sliced corned beef, shredded
~ 3 cups milk
~ 12 ounces Swiss cheese, shredded
~ salt and pepper

In a stockpot, melt the butter over medium heat. Add the onion and celery and sauté until the onion begins to color, about 5 minutes. Stir in the stock and tapioca and remove from heat; let the mixture stand for 5 minutes. Put the soup back on the stove and bring to a boil over medium heat, stirring frequently. Reduce the heat, uncover, and simmer 5 minutes longer. Stir in the sauerkraut and corned beef. Add the milk and 1 cup shredded Swiss cheese. Cook and stir frequently for 30 minutes until slightly thickened. Season with salt and pepper to taste. Preheat the broiler. To serve, ladle soup into 8 ovenproof bowls; top each one with several pieces of the toasted bread. Sprinkle with remaining cheese. Place under the broiler until cheese is melted. Serve immediately.

Sauerkraut Tomato Soup

~ 2 pounds sauerkraut
~ 1 (28 oz) can whole tomatoes, undrained
~ 1 cup chopped onions
~ 1 (13 ¾ oz) can chicken broth
~ 1 ½ cups water, or as needed
~ salt and pepper
~ cooked shrimp for garnish

Drain sauerkraut well, reserving juice and about ½ cup sauerkraut for garnish. Combine sauerkraut, tomatoes, onions, and broth in stainless steel pot or Dutch oven. Bring to a boil. Cover and simmer over low heat 2 ½ - 3 hours. Add water as needed during cooking. Season with some of the reserved juice. Garnish with cooked shrimp and reserved sauerkraut. Serve with rye bread. Serves 6-8.

Sauerkraut Sausage Soup

~ 1 pound sausage with sage
~ ½ cup chopped onion
~ 2 garlic cloves, minced
~ 1 pound sauerkraut, undrained
~ 3 (16 oz) cans chicken broth
~ 1 ½ tbsp butter
~ 1 ½ tbsp all-purpose flour
~ 1 tsp sugar

In a large stock pot, over low heat, sauté the sausage, onion, and garlic until the sausage, is brown, 7-10 minutes. Drain off the fat and discard. Add the sauerkraut and broth. Cook, covered for 40 minutes. In a small saucepan, over medium-low heat, melt the butter. Stir in the flour (with a whisk) cooking just until it bubbles. Then pour in 1 cup of the soup stock and whisk together. Return this mixture to the stock pot. Raise the heat to medium; stir and cook about 10 minutes or until it thickens. Add sugar, blend well, then add to soup bowls. Serve.

Polish Sauerkraut Soup
(see next page for Potato Dumplings recipe)

~ 2 pounds smoked pork shanks
~ 1 quart water
~ 1 large onion, well browned
~ 1 quart sauerkraut, drained
~ 2 tsp salt
~ ¼ cup cream
~ 1 egg
~ 1 tbsp flour
~ ¾ cup milk

Cook meat in water until well done. Add onion, sauerkraut, and salt. Combine in a separate bowl: beaten egg, flour, milk, and cream. Add mixture to soup and bring to boiling point. Serve with potato dumplings – recipe follows. Serves 4-6.

Potato Dumplings

~ 1 egg slightly beaten
~ 2 cups flour
~ 2 cups left over mashed potatoes
~ 1 tsp salt

In a large mixing bowl, place the measured mashed potatoes with equal amount of flour. Add the slightly beaten egg, salt, and mix thoroughly with your hand until the mixture holds together. Form into small balls about 2 inches in diameter. In a 2 quart saucepan, fill with water and heat to boiling. Drop potato balls into boiling water. Make certain that the water continues to boil and completely covers the dumplings. The dumplings are cooked when they float. Remove from the water and serve with any pork dish and sauerkraut.

Salads

Hot German Potato Salad

- ~ 5 medium red potatoes
- ~ 6 slices bacon
- ~ ½ cup medium onion, chopped
- ~ 1 cup sauerkraut, drained
- ~ ¼ cup water
- ~ ½ cup apple cider vinegar
- ~ 1 tsp pepper
- ~ 2 tbsp parsley, chopped

In a large pot, boil potatoes with peeling until tender. Drain and cool. Peel potatoes and cut into large diced pieces. In a 10 inch frying pan, cook bacon until crisp, Drain bacon on paper towels, reserving drippings. Cut bacon into ½ inch pieces. Sauté onions in the bacon fat until translucent. Add water and vinegar to deglaze the pan. Bring to a boil. Stir in sauerkraut, potatoes, and chopped bacon. Season with salt and pepper. Heat through. Remove from heat and stir in parsley. Serve immediately. Serves 2-4.

Sauerkraut Potato Salad

~ 3 ½ cups sauerkraut, drained
~ 6 cups diced cooked potatoes
~ 2 hard boiled eggs, chopped
~ 2 large onions, diced
~ ¾ cup mayonnaise
~ 12 tsp paprika
~ salt and pepper to taste

Combine sauerkraut, potatoes, eggs, and onions. Toss lightly. Add remaining ingredients. Toss lightly and chill. You may also add diced green peppers and celery.

Reuben Macaroni Salad

~ 1 ½ cups elbow macaroni
~ ½ pounds corned beef, diced
~ 1 cup Swiss cheese, shredded
~ 2 cups sauerkraut, drained
~ ½ tsp caraway seed
~ ⅔ cup bottled Russian dressing
~ 2 tomatoes, cut into wedges

Cook macaroni until tender; drain and cool. In a large bowl, combine the corned beef, cheese, sauerkraut, caraway seed, and Russian dressing. Add cooked macaroni, and toss thoroughly. Serve with tomato wedges. Serves 4.

Variation: You may also mix in a can of kidney beans, rinsed and drained, to the recipe, if desired.

Sauerkraut Slaw

~ 1 green pepper
~ 1 cup diced onion
~ 1 cup diced celery
~ 1 cup sugar
~ 1 can (24 oz) sauerkraut

Mix all ingredients together. This tastes much better if made a day ahead of time. 3 servings.

Summer Kraut Salad

~ 4 cups sauerkraut, rinsed and drained
~ ½ cup sliced onions
~ 1 cup diced celery
~ 1 ¾ cup seedless red grapes, halved
~ 2 cups unpeeled red apple, diced
~ 3 tbsp apple cider vinegar
~ 3 tbsp lemon juice
~ 3 tbsp honey
~ 2 tbsp olive oil
~ salt and pepper

Place sauerkraut in large bowl. Add onion, celery, grapes, and apple. In a small bowl, blend vinegar, lemon juice, and honey; gradually whisk in oil; pour dressing over salad and toss until well combined. Add salt and pepper to taste. Refrigerate for at least 1 hour or until serving time. Serves 8.

Tangy 3 Bean Salad

~ 2 cups frozen French cut green beans
~ 1 can (15 oz) chickpeas, drained
~ 1 can (15 oz) red kidney beans, drained
~ 1 cup sauerkraut, drained
~ ½ cup red bell pepper, chopped
~ ½ cup raspberry vinaigrette
~ salt to taste

Cook green beans according to package directions, Drain; rinse with cold water. In large bowl, stir together cooled beans and all remaining ingredients. Serve immediately, or refrigerate overnight to blend flavors.

Waldorf Sauerkraut Salad

~ 2 cups sauerkraut
~ 3 green onions, chopped
~ 1 green pepper, chopped
~ 1 cup grated carrot
~ ½ cup chopped celery
~ 3 large red apples, unpeeled, cored, and diced
~ ½ tsp salt
~ ⅓ cup sugar
~ ½ tsp celery seed
~ ⅓ cup white vinegar
~ ⅓ cup canola oil
~ ½ cup walnuts, chopped

Rinse and drain sauerkraut thoroughly. In a glass bowl, mix sauerkraut, apples, and vegetables. Combine salt, sugar, celery seed, vinegar, and oil. Pour over sauerkraut mixture. Cover and refrigerate 4-6 hours. Mix thoroughly and drain before serving. Sprinkle with nuts as desired. Makes 6-8 servings.

Sauerkraut Apple Salad

~ ½ pound sauerkraut
~ 3 tbsp olive oil
~ 2 apples, grated
~ 1 onion, chopped
~ 1 tsp sugar
~ salt and pepper

Drain sauerkraut. Make marinate of remaining ingredients. Add to sauerkraut. Let stand 15 minutes before serving. This salad goes well with fish. Serves 4.

Pistachio Sauerkraut Salad

~ 14 ounces sauerkraut, drained
~ 1 ounce pkg instant pistachio pudding mix
~ 2 tsp fresh lemon rind
~ ½ cup coarsely chopped pistachios
~ ½ cup coarsely chopped pecans
~ ¼ cup dried cranberries
~ 1 tbsp honey

Drain the sauerkraut and place in a large bowl. Fill the bowl with water and rinse with pickling juices from the sauerkraut; then drain using a large colander with small holes. Put the sauerkraut back into the bowl, refill it with cool water, and set it aside. Make the pudding according to package directions. When it has begun to set, add the lemon rind. Coarsely chop the pistachios and pecans. Pour the sauerkraut into the colander again and drain it well, pressing it down with the back of a spatula. In a large bowl, mix the rinsed/drained sauerkraut with pudding, nuts, cranberries, and honey. Stir well. Pour into a serving container and chill in refrigerator for at least one hour before serving. Enjoy!

Sauerkraut and Avocado Salad

~ 1 cup sauerkraut, undrained
~ 1 plum, chopped fine
~ ½ sliced avocado
~ 2 tbsp garbanzo beans
~ ½ cup soaked romaine lettuce
~ 1 cup water
~ 1 tbsp soy sauce
~ ½ cup chopped parsley
~ ½ cup sliced scallions

Mix sauerkraut and plum together lightly. Place in wet salad bowl. Spread slices of avocado over sauerkraut mixture. Sprinkle garbanzo beans around this, sprinkle romaine lettuce on top. Pour water over vegetables. Sprinkle soy sauce over vegetables. Let set 10-15 minutes. Refrigerate for at least 30 minutes. Turn out salad on plate. Garnish with parsley and scallions. Serves 4.

Tropical Fruit Salad

~ 1 ripe mango
~ 1 can (15.25 oz) pineapple tidbits with juice
~ 1 cup sauerkraut, drained and rinsed
~ 1 jar (6 oz) maraschino cherries, drained

Washed and peel mango. Cut flesh away from seed and cut into ½ inch cubes. In a large bowl, combine mango cubes, pineapple with juice, sauerkraut, and cherries. Mix well. Chill before serving. Serves 6.

Spring Sauerkraut and Fruit Salad

~ 3 cups sauerkraut, drained (reserve juice for marinade)
~ 1 medium red delicious apple, chopped
~ 1 medium orange, peeled, sectioned, and chopped
~ ¼ cup finely chopped celery
~ ¼ cup orange juice
~ 1 tbsp sugar
~ 1 tbsp chopped chives

Toss kraut, apple, orange, celery, and orange juice. Mix well with sugar and chives. Chill until ready to serve. Serves 4 to 6.

Sauerkraut Spaghetti Salad

~ ½ pound raw spaghetti, cut into 2 inch pieces
~ 4 cups sauerkraut, drained and lightly rinsed
~ ½ cup green bell peppers, thinly julienned
~ ¼ cup pimentos
~ 1 cup carrots, peeled and grated
~ 1 ½ tbsp parsley, chopped

Dressing:
~ 3 oz cider vinegar
~ 3 oz vegetable oil
~ 3 oz water
~ 3 oz sugar
~ 1 tsp dried oregano
~ 1 tsp dried mustard
~ 1 tsp granulated sugar
~ 1 tsp salt
~ ½ tsp ground black pepper

Cook spaghetti in boiling water until tender (about 12 minutes). Drain, but do not rinse; let cool. In mixing bowl, combine spaghetti, sauerkraut, green peppers, pimentos, carrots, and parsley.

For the Dressing: Combine all dressing ingredients together in a mixing bowl or blender and whisk or blend together. Toss salad ingredients with dressing and serve immediately or refrigerate overnight to blend flavors. Servings: 8-10.

Sauerkraut Salad with Ham

~ 1 pound sauerkraut
~ ½ pound grapes, seedless
~ 6 ounces ham, cooked

Dressing:
~ ½ cup yogurt
~ ¼ tsp salt
~ ¼ tsp white pepper
~ 1 tsp honey

Rinse and drain sauerkraut. Chop coarsely. Wash grapes and cut in half. Cut ham in strips. Gently mix these 3 ingredients. Blend dressing, ingredients, and stir into sauerkraut mixture. Marinate for 10 minutes; adjust seasoning before serving, if necessary.

Curried Chicken Salad

~ 1 cup sauerkraut, chopped, (light rinsed, excess moisture squeezed out)
~ 1 cup green and red grapes, halved
~ ¾ cup finely chopped celery
~ ½ cup finely chopped sweet onion
~ ½ cup sliced almonds
~ ½ tsp curry powder
~ ½ tsp poultry seasoning
~ ¾ cup mayonnaise
~ 2 cans (10 oz each) cooked chicken, drained

In a large bowl, combine first 5 ingredients. Add seasonings and mix well. Add mayonnaise and mix well. Fold in chicken. Serves 6.

Chicken and Sauerkraut Salad with Basil-Orange Vinaigrette

- ~ 1 tsp crushed fennel seeds
- ~ 1 tsp Dijon mustard
- ~ 1 clove garlic
- ~ 2 tsp grated orange zest
- ~ 2 tbsp balsamic vinegar
- ~ 2 tbsp olive oil
- ~ ½ cup fresh basil
- ~ ½ tsp pepper
- ~ ¾ pound cooked chicken breasts, cut into ¼ inch strips
- ~ 1 pound rinsed and thoroughly drained sauerkraut
- ~ salt and pepper
- ~ 8 romaine lettuce leaves
- ~ 2 small pita bread rounds cut in half

To make dressing: Combine fennel seeds, mustard, garlic, orange zest, vinegar, olive oil, basil, and pepper. Set aside.

Toss chicken strips with sauerkraut and half the dressing. Add salt and pepper to taste. On each of four plates, place 2 romaine lettuce leaves and top with salad. Add remaining dressing to each plate. Serve with pita bread pieces. Serves 4.

Reuben Salad

~ 1 large head lettuce
~ ¾ pound cooked, lean corned beef, cut into strips
~ 2 cups sauerkraut, rinsed and drained
~ ½ pounds Swiss cheese, cubed (2 cups)
~ 1 cup Russian dressing
~ 1 cup pumpernickel crumbs (recipe follows)
~ 1 tsp caraway seeds

Tear lettuce into a large bowl. (Should make 6 cups), reserving 4 large leaves to garnish plates. Add corned beef, sauerkraut, and Swiss Cheese; toss gently. Divide mixture evenly and place on top of whole lettuce leaves on plate. Pour on Russian dressing; top with croutons and sprinkle with caraway seeds.

Pumpernickel Croutons

~ 3 tbsp butter
~ 4 slices pumpernickel bread

Spread butter on all slices of pumpernickel bread. Cut into ½ inch cubes. Bake 15 minutes on a baking sheet at 300 degrees. Set aside when done, to cool. Sprinkle over Reuben Salad. Serves 4.

Sauerkraut Jell-o

~ 1 small packet of Jell-o (any flavor)
~ 1 ½ cups sauerkraut
~ 1 cup cooked carrots
~ 1 tsp water

Make jell-o according to package. Before jell-o firms, add sauerkraut, carrots and water. Let it firm and enjoy. It's lovely.

Main Dishes
and Casseroles

German Sauerkraut

~ 2 pounds cabbage
~ 3 tbsp butter
~ 1 onion, chopped
~ 1 apple, sliced
~ salt and pepper
~ 1 potato, raw
~ ⅓ cup cream
~ sugar and paprika to taste

Pluck apart cabbage and wash well. Shred. Melt butter in a fairly large pot and turn cabbage in it thoroughly. Add onion, apple, and salt and pepper to taste. Fill pot with water. Cook until tender, about 10 minutes. Grate into this raw potato, to give a nice texture. Add cream; add sugar and paprika to taste. Serves 4.

German Sauerkraut Casserole

~ 1 pound sauerkraut
~ 1 cup sugar
~ 6 slices bacon
~ 1 tsp black pepper

Mix sauerkraut, pepper, and sugar together in 1 ½ quart dish. Cut bacon slices in 1 inch pieces and mix slightly with sauerkraut. Bake at 325 degrees for 2 ¼ hours.

German Sauerkraut Puff-Pie

~ Puff pie crust (recipe follows)
~ 1 ½ pounds cooked sauerkraut, dry
~ ½ pound frankfurters, lightly fried
~ ½ pound bacon, lightly fried
~ 1 cup milk
~ 3 tbsp tomato sauce
~ t tbsp paprika
~ 1 egg yolk

Prepare Puff-pie crust dough. Grease a baking dish and line with two thirds of dough. Arrange alternate layers of cooked sauerkraut, frankfurters, and bacon. Mix together milk, tomato sauce, and paprika and pour over casserole. Roll out remaining dough to fit across top of pie. Prick with fork (on top) wide air holes, or dough can be cut into strips and laid on top in any desired pattern. Brush top of dough with egg yolk. Bake in moderate 350 degree oven for one hour. Serves 4.

Puff-pie crust

~ ¾ pound butter
~ 2 cups flour
~ 1 egg
~ 2 tbsp water
~ pinch of salt

Melt butter and work in all other ingredients to make a smooth firm dough. Roll out and use in recipe.

Pork Roast and Sauerkraut

~ 1 pork roast (4 pounds)
~ 1 large can sauerkraut (32 oz)
~ 2 large cooking apples, chopped
~ ¼ cup brown sugar

Mix sauerkraut, apples, and brown sugar. Place in bottom of roasting pan; put pork roast on top. Cover. Bake at 350 degrees for 4-5 hours. Serves 12.

Pork Loin with Sauerkraut and Beets

~ 2 pound center cut boneless pork loin
~ Dry rub (see recipe below)
~ 1 can (15 oz) whole beets, drained with juice reserved
~ ½ cup water
~ 2 cups sauerkraut, drained

Dry Rub: Mix together 1 tbsp each: coarse salt, dry mustard, and freshly ground pepper.

Preheat oven to 350 degrees. Press dry rub onto surface of meat; roast in roasting pan for 40 minutes or until juice runs clear (to 150 degrees). Transfer meat to a large platter and allow to rest 15 minutes before slicing. Meanwhile, pour half of the beet juice into the roasting pan; add water. Over medium heat, boil juices about 5 minutes, stirring to loosen meat pieces on pan bottom. Reserve 6 beets for garnish and puree the remaining beets in a blender; add juices from pan. Set aside. Combine sauerkraut and remaining beet juice in saucepan and simmer until juice is absorbed. Place the 6 reserved beets on top of the kraut to warm. Cut pork into 12 slices. Divide pureed beet and juice mixture among 6 plates. Top each 'puddle' of sauce with 2 slices of pork. Divide kraut mixture among plates. Slice 6 beets and fan one on each plate. Serves 6.

Pork Chops with Sauerkraut and Potatoes

~ 2 medium onions, coarsely chopped
~ 6 ¾ inch fresh or smoked pork chops, well trimmed
~ coarsely ground black pepper
~ 6 small potatoes, peeled, chunked, and precooked (see note)
~ 2 (15 oz) cans sauerkraut, well drained
~ 2 (15 oz) cans low fat chicken broth
~ 9 whole cloves

Preheat oven to 300 degrees. Coat a large Dutch oven with non-stick cooking spray. Sprinkle half the onions in the bottom of the pan. Place the pork chops on top; sprinkle with pepper; arrange potatoes around pork chops. Top with sauerkraut, then pour the stock over all. Drop in whole cloves. Cover and bake for 2 hours. Serve hot in deep-lipped plates adding some stock to each serving.

Note: To precook the potatoes, place the peeled chunks in a 9x9 inch dish; add 1 cup water or stock, cover and microwave on high for 6-7 minutes, stirring after 3 minutes. Alternatively, simmering in salted water for 6-8 minutes. The potatoes should be a bit done and will finish baking in the oven with the meat, kraut, and all those good pan juices.

Smoked Pork Chops with Sauerkraut and Apples

~ 3 tbsp olive oil
~ ½ pound thick sliced bacon, cut into very small squares
~ 2 yellow onions, halved and sliced crosswise
~ 2 cloves fresh garlic, chopped
~ 2 pounds refrigerated prepared sauerkraut, rinsed
~ 2 small granny smith apples, peeled and grated
~ 1 boiling potato, peeled and grated
~ 1 cup chicken broth
~ ½ cup apple cider
~ ½ tsp dried thyme
~ 1 bay leaf
~ 2 whole cloves
~ 2 pounds smoked pork chops, ½ - ¾ inch thick

In a Dutch oven or casserole, heat olive oil over medium heat. Add the bacon and sauté until browned, about 8 minutes. Using a slotted spoon, remove bacon to plate. Add the onions to the pot and sauté until softened, about 6 minutes. Add the garlic and sauté 1 minute. Add the sauerkraut, grated apples, and grated potato; sauté 2 minutes. Add the chicken broth, cider, thyme, bay leaf, and cloves. Bring to a simmer and cook uncovered, for 30 minutes. Tuck the pork chops and bacon into sauerkraut mixture. Cover pot and simmer until port chops are heated through and done, usually about 30 minutes. Serves 8.

Pork Chops with Sauerkraut and Pineapple

~ 6 pork chops
~ 2 tbsp olive oil
~ 1 (27 oz) can sauerkraut, drained and rinsed
~ 1 (20 oz) can crushed pineapple
~ 2 tbsp brown sugar
~ ½ tsp salt
~ ¼ tsp pepper
~ ½ cup chopped onion

Brown pork chops in oil. Remove and put in casserole dish. Cover with kraut, pineapple, onion, brown sugar, salt, and pepper. Bake, covered, 45 minutes at 350 degrees.

Super Sized Kraut Stuffed Pork Chops

~ 1 cup butter, divided
~ 6 thick-cut pork chops
~ 2 green peppers, divided
~ 1 cup diced onion
~ 1 bag (10 oz) shredded carrots
~ 6 cups (48 oz) sauerkraut, drained
~ 1 tbsp sugar
~ 1 ½ tsp salt
~ ¼ tsp pepper
~ ¼ tsp dried thyme

In a large skillet, melt ¼ cup butter. Add pork chops. Cook until browned on both sides. Remove chops and set aside. Reserve drippings. Slice 4 rings from green peppers and set aside. Dice remaining green pepper. Add remaining ¾ cup butter to drippings in skillet; melt butter. Add diced pepper, onion and sauté, stirring constantly, until crisp-tender. Stir in carrots; sauté 1 minute. Add sauerkraut, salt, sugar, pepper, and thyme; toss until combined. With sharp knife, cut each pork chop horizontally at fat side to bone to form a pocket. Stuff each pork chop with vegetable mixture. Bake until internal temperature reaches 160 degrees. Serves 6.

Sauerkraut Marinated Pork Kabobs

~ ½ cup sauerkraut juice (reserve sauerkraut)
~ ½ cup olive oil
~ ¼ cup apple cider vinegar
~ ¼ cup soy sauce
~ 2 tsp Worcestershire sauce
~ 2 small onions, thinly sliced
~ 2 whole cloves garlic, crushed
~ 1 tsp coarsely ground black pepper
~ 1 tsp dry mustard
~ 1 ½ pounds pork shoulder, cubed

Combine sauerkraut juice, olive oil, vinegar, soy sauce, Worcestershire sauce, onions, garlic, pepper, and dry mustard in a bowl; add pork cubes to marinate and turn to coat thoroughly. Cover and marinate 6 hours in refrigerator. Remove meat from marinade, thread on skewers, and grill on high heat for one minute. Reduce heat to medium and cook 10-12 minutes, turning once. Heat reserved sauerkraut. Serve kabobs with sauerkraut and a variety of grilled vegetables. Serves 8. (2 ounces each).

Barbequed Pork with Sauerkraut

~ Pork roast
~ 1 (15 oz) can sauerkraut
~ 1 (8oz) can tomato sauce
~ ½ cup thick, zesty barbeque sauce
~ 2 tbsp honey
~ 1 tbsp cornstarch
~ salt and pepper to taste

Salt and pepper pork and place in roasting pan with 1 cup water. Roast in 325 degree oven for 2-3 hours until done. In a mixing bowl, add tomato sauce, barbeque sauce, honey, and cornstarch. Stir until well blended. Set aside. When pork is done, remove from oven and slice into serving portions. Drain juices from roasting pan, place pork back in roasting pan, place pork back in roasting pan, and pour sauce mixture evenly over pork. Arrange sauerkraut on top of sauce. Cover pan and bake in 325 degree oven for ½ hour. Serves 4-6.

Pork Hocks and Sauerkraut (Ham Hocks)

~ 6-9 Pork Hocks
~ 3 cups sauerkraut
~ 1 cup sauerkraut juice
~ 2-4 medium to large onions, sliced
~ Celery seed

Place pork hocks in a 2-3 quart casserole dish. Cover with sauerkraut. Add juice and water. Put sliced onions on top and sprinkle with celery seed. Cover dish tightly and bake at 350 degrees for 3-4 hours. Serve with mustard and horseradish.

Sauerkraut Pork Stew

~ 6 boneless center cut pork chops
~ 1 (32 oz) can sauerkraut
~ 2 onions, sliced thin
~ 4 apples, peeled and sliced
~ ½ cup milk
~ salt and pepper

Preheat oven to 300 degrees. Sprinkle chops with salt and pepper. In Dutch oven, layer half of the chops, top with half of the sauerkraut, then half of the onions, then half of the apples. Repeat. Pour milk over mixture. Cover and bake in 300 degree oven for 3 ½ hours.

Baked Spareribs and Sauerkraut with Dumplings
(see next page for Potato Dumplings recipe)

~ spareribs
~ sauerkraut
~ 2 cups flour
~ 1 egg beaten
~ 1 tsp baking powder
~ 1 cup milk

Cut spareribs into serving portions and place in the bottom of roasting pan. Add the sauerkraut and a little liquid. Cover and bake in moderate oven, 350 degrees, 1 ½ hours.

Make dumplings by combining flour, baking powder, milk and egg. Drop by spoonfuls onto sauerkraut. Cover tightly and bake for 20 minutes at 350 degrees.

Substitution: You may also substitute potato dumplings for regular dumplings. Recipe follows for potato dumplings.

Potato Dumplings

~   1 egg slightly beaten
~   2 cups flour
~   2 cups left over mashed potatoes
~   1 tsp salt

In a large mixing bowl, place the measured mashed potatoes with equal amount of flour. Add the slightly beaten egg, salt, and mix thoroughly with your hand until the mixture holds together. Form into small balls about 2 inches in diameter. In a 2 quart saucepan, fill with water and heat to boiling. Drop potato balls into boiling water. Make certain that the water continues to boil and completely covers the dumplings. The dumplings are cooked when they float. Remove from the water and serve with any pork dish and sauerkraut.

Spareribs and Sauerkraut

~ 1 quart water
~ 6 pounds spareribs
~ 3 cups sauerkraut
~ salt and pepper

Bring water to a boil. Add meat, sauerkraut, and seasoning. Stew for about 1 ½ hours. Serve with any kind of potatoes. Serves 4.

German Pork and Sauerkraut

- ~ 2 pounds pork ribs
- ~ 1 medium onion, chopped
- ~ 1 tbsp cooking oil
- ~ 1 (14 oz) can sauerkraut
- ~ 1 cup applesauce
- ~ 2 tbsp brown sugar
- ~ 2 tsp caraway seeds
- ~ 1 tsp garlic powder
- ~ ½ tsp pepper

In a Dutch oven, cook ribs and onions until ribs are browned and onion is tender. Remove from heat. Combine remaining ingredients and pour over ribs. Cover and bake in oven at 350 degrees for 1 ½ - 2 hours or until ribs are tender (or place in crock pot and cook on low 8 hours).

Meatball and Sauerkraut Meal

~ 1 ½ pound hamburger
~ 2 onions, chopped
~ 2 (8oz) cans tomato sauce
~ 1 pound sauerkraut
~ ¼ cup rice
~ ½ cup brown sugar

Mix hamburger, rice and onions, to make meatballs; brown in skillet. In crock pot stir together tomato sauce, brown sugar and sauerkraut. Add meatballs and cook in crock pot on low 6-8 hours.

Sauerkraut Meatloaf

~ 1 (16 oz) can sauerkraut
~ 1 medium onion, diced
~ 1 tbsp, butter
~ 2 eggs
~ ⅓ cup milk
~ 1 tbsp mustard
~ 1 tsp salt
~ 1 tsp thyme
~ ⅛ tsp pepper
~ 1 pound ground chuck
~ 1 pound sausage
~ 2 cups rye bread crumbs
~ ⅓ cup catsup
~ ⅓ cup brown sugar

Drain kraut well and snip up fine. Sauté onion in butter until soft. Beat eggs slightly in large bowl; stir in milk, mustard, salt, pepper, and thyme. Add sauerkraut, onion mixture, ground chuck, sausage, and bread crumbs. Mix well. Shape into loaves. Mix catsup and brown sugar in bowl; set aside. Bake loaves at 350 degrees for 1 hour. Baste with catsup mixture after 45 minutes.

Baked Tomato Sauerkraut

~ 1 pound ground beef
~ 1 medium onion, chopped
~ 1 pound sauerkraut, drained very well
~ ½ cup dark brown sugar, packed
~ 1 cup (10 oz) tomato puree
~ 1 small bay leaf, halved
~ ¼ tsp salt
~ ¼ tsp ground black pepper

Preheat oven to 350 degrees. In a deep saucepan, over medium heat, sauté meat and onion together until the meat begins to brown, 5-10 minutes. Drain off any excess fat. Stir in the sauerkraut, brown sugar, tomato puree, bay left, salt and pepper. Transfer to a greased shallow 2 quart casserole and bake for 35-45 minutes or until bubbling in the middle. Remove the bay leaf and serve immediately.

Baked Hamburger Sauerkraut

~ 1 pound hamburger
~ 1 egg
~ 2 tbsp flour
~ ½ cup chopped onion
~ salt and pepper to taste
~ 3 tbsp olive oil
~ 3 cups sauerkraut
~ ¼ cup catsup

Combine hamburger, egg, flour, onion, salt and pepper. Brown in olive oil. Alternate layers of meat mixture and kraut in 1 quart casserole bowl. Dot top with catsup. Bake in 350 degree oven about 1 hour. Serves 6.

Baked Sauerkraut

~ 1 (16 oz) can sauerkraut, drained well
~ ½ cup raisins
~ 2 tsp brown sugar

Mix ingredients together. Heat in 350 degree oven until brown. Serve with pork chops, ham or sausage.

Sauerkraut Perogies

- ~ 2 cups all purpose flour
- ~ 1 tsp salt
- ~ 1 egg, beaten
- ~ ⅔ cup cold water
- ~ 1 ¼ pound bacon
- ~ 5 pounds baking potatoes
- ~ 1 cup shredded cheddar cheese
- ~ salt and pepper to taste
- ~ 1 (32 oz) jar sauerkraut, drained, rinsed and minced
- ~ 3 tbsp sour cream

To make dough: In a medium bowl, combine the flour, salt, egg, and water. Mix all together to form dough, cover bowl and set aside.

To make potato filling: Place potatoes in a large pot. Add water to cover; bring to a boil for 25-25 minutes or until tender. Remove potatoes from water and mash. Place 1 pound of bacon in a large, deep skillet. Cover over medium high heat until evenly brown; drain; crumble and stir into mashed potatoes. Stir in cheese and season with salt and pepper.

To make sauerkraut filling: Place ¼ pound bacon in a large deep skillet. Cover over medium high heat until evenly brown. Drain, crumble, and place in a medium bowl. Stir in sauerkraut and sour cream. Mix well.

Roll reserved dough out on a floured surface. Cut circles out of dough, using a small round container. Place a spoonful of potato or sauerkraut filling in the center of each circle and fold over, pinching edges together to seal. Bring a large pot of salted water to a boil; drop perogies in boiling water and cook for 4-5 minutes or until they float. Remove; put on plate and serve. Great snack or appetizer!

Bacon Fried Sauerkraut

~ 2-4 tbsp butter
~ 2 cups sauerkraut, drained
~ salt and pepper
~ 3 slices bacon, fried and crumbled

Melt butter in frying pan. Add drained sauerkraut. Sprinkle with salt and pepper. Sauté until browned. Add the crumbled bacon. Simmer on medium low heat for 5 minutes. Serve.

Substitution: You may substitute 4 cut up hotdogs instead of bacon, if desired.

Sauerkraut and Sausage Croquettes

~ ½ pound pork sausage
~ 2 ½ tbsp dehydrated onion, minced
~ 8 ounces sauerkraut, drained and chopped
~ 2 tbsp plain dry bread crumbs
~ 1 (3 oz) pkg cream cheese, softened
~ 1 tsp stone ground mustard
~ 1 clove garlic, pressed
~ ¼ tsp black pepper
~ 2 eggs well beaten
~ 1 cup plain dry bread crumbs

Brown sausage with minced onions in a skillet until done. Drain and add sauerkraut and 2 tbsp bread crumbs. Combine cream cheese, mustard, garlic, and pepper in a bowl and mix well. Stir into sausage mixture and stir until thoroughly mixed. Refrigerate. Form into small balls, dip into egg, then dip into bread crumbs. Coat with bread crumbs, fry until golden brown. Just before serving, bake at 375 degrees for 15-20 minutes.

Corned Beef Sauerkraut Casserole

~ 32 oz pkg sauerkraut, drained
~ 4 oz pkg dry noodles
~ ½ cup dried onions
~ 2 cans (10 ¾ oz each) cream of mushroom soup
~ 1 cup milk
~ 3 tbsp mustard
~ 2 (4 oz) pkgs grated Swiss cheese
~ 1 (12 oz) can corned beef

Put drained sauerkraut into a greased 9x13 inch pan. Spread with uncooked noodles. Mix onion, soup, milk and mustard together and pour over noodles. Break corned beef apart and put over top of above. Sprinkle Swiss cheese on top. Cover with foil and bake at 350 degrees for 1 hour.

Sauerkraut Shepherd's Pie

~ 1 pound hamburger, browned and seasoned
~ 1 (15 oz) can sauerkraut
~ 3 cups mashed potatoes
~ 1 tbsp butter
~ paprika

Brown hamburger and place in 1 ½ quart casserole. Warm sauerkraut in saucepan with 1 tablespoon butter. Drain kraut and place over hamburger in casserole dish. Cook and mash 3 cups mashed potatoes. Place mashed potatoes on top of sauerkraut. Dot with butter and paprika. Bake at 350 degrees for 30 minutes. Serves 4.

Bavarian Patties with Sauerkraut

~ 1 ½ pounds ground beef
~ ½ cup applesauce
~ ⅓ cup dry bread crumbs
~ 1 small onion, finely chopped
~ 1 egg
~ 1 tsp salt
~ ½ tsp allspice
~ 1 (15 oz) can sauerkraut, drained

Mix all ingredients together except sauerkraut. Shape mixture into 6 patties. Brown patties in a large skillet over medium heat, turning once. Drain off fat. Spoon sauerkraut over patties, cover and simmer 15 minutes.

Rolled Flank Steak

~ 1 flank steak
~ 1 tsp ground pepper
~ ½ tsp crushed bay leaf
~ 1 tsp crushed savory
~ 2 tbsp minced onion
~ 1 can (16 oz) sauerkraut
~ 2-3 cups mashed potatoes

Pound flank steak, rub with pepper on one side then on the other side rub on the bay leafs, savory, and onion. Cover meat – first with sauerkraut (save juice for basting) then mashed potatoes. Roll steak and secure. Bake or broil till the meat is cooked to your desired temperature. Baste with kraut juice.

Sauerkraut Rolls

- ~ 4 pieces of steak (elk or deer)
- ~ 2 slices bacon
- ~ ½ onion, chopped
- ~ 2 tsp sugar
- ~ ¼ tsp pepper
- ~ 1 cup sauerkraut
- ~ ½ cup meat stock

Pound meat quite thin and cut into pieces about 4 x 4 inches. Dice bacon and fry; add onion and cook 5 minutes. Add sugar, pepper, and sauerkraut. Heat thoroughly. Place a portion of sauerkraut mixture in center of each piece of meat. Roll and tie securely with thread or a fine string. Place rolls in a greased casserole dish and add meat stock. Bake in moderate oven at 350 degrees about 1 hour or until meat is tender.

Barbequed Sauerkraut

~ 1 ½ pounds hamburger
~ 1 medium onion, chopped
~ 1 (15 oz) can tomato sauce
~ 1 cup brown sugar
~ 1 quart sauerkraut

Lightly brown hamburger and medium onion. Add tomato sauce, brown sugar, and sauerkraut. Put into a baking dish. Bake 1 ½ hours at 350 degrees uncovered.

Baked Hen with Sauerkraut Stuffing

~ ¾ cup shopped onion
~ ½ stick butter
~ 4 cups sauerkraut, drained
~ 2 tart apples, peeled and chopped
~ ½ cup chopped celery
~ 1 tbsp caraway seed
~ salt and pepper to taste
~ 1 (3 pound) hen
~ 1 tbsp butter

To make sauerkraut stuffing: In a large skillet, sauté onion in butter until slightly browned. Add sauerkraut, apples, celery, and caraway seed, salt, and pepper. Cook the mixture over moderately high heat, tossing it for 5 minutes. Let cool to room temperature.

Sprinkle hen inside and out with salt and pepper. Pack cavity with sauerkraut stuffing. Truss the hen and rub with softened butter. Put hen in buttered casserole and surround it with the remaining stuffing. Braise the hen, covered, in a 350 degree oven for 2 hours. Remove the lid and roast the hen, basting it occasionally in the pan juices for another 45 minutes or until hen is tender and slightly browned. Serve with mashed potatoes.

Sauerkraut and Chicken Stir Fry

~ 1 tsp soy sauce
~ 2 tbsp cornstarch
~ ½ tbsp finely chopped garlic
~ 1 whole, uncooked, skinless, boneless chicken breast (approximately ¾ pound) cut into bite sized pieces
~ 2 tbsp corn oil
~ ⅓ cup julienned red peppers
~ ⅓ cup julienned green peppers
~ ⅓ cup julienned snow peas
~ ⅓ cup julienned carrots
~ 1 pound sauerkraut, drained
~ 2 scallions, sliced
~ 1 cup unsalted cashews

Combine soy sauce, cornstarch and garlic in small bowl; set aside. Heat oil in large non-stick skillet over medium high heat; add chicken and soy sauce mixture. Sauté stirring continuously until cooked through. Remove chicken with a slotted spoon. Add peppers, snow peas, and carrots to skillet. Cook stirring continuously about 3 minutes. Add sauerkraut and stir until heated through. Stir in cooked chicken and scallions and sauté 2 minutes more. Sprinkle with cashews and serve immediately. Serves 4.

Chicken and Sauerkraut Bake

~ 8 chicken breasts, skinless, boneless
~ 1 (16 oz) jar sauerkraut
~ 1 cup rice
~ 1 envelope dry onion soup mix
~ 1 cup water

Place sauerkraut in 9x13 pan, sprinkle on rice. Put chicken on top of sauerkraut and rice. Sprinkle on soup mix and water; cover with foil. Bake at 350 degrees for about 2 hours; uncover the last 15 minutes.

Frankfurter and Sauerkraut Bake

~ 2 cups sauerkraut, drained
~ 2 medium apples, cored and diced
~ 1 tsp caraway seeds
~ ¼ tsp ground cloves
~ pepper to taste
~ 2 tbsp butter, melted
~ 8 frankfurters

In shallow 9x12 baking pan, combine sauerkraut, apples, caraway seeds, cloves, and pepper. Add butter. Stir to mix well. Arrange frankfurters on top. Bake in 350 degree oven for 30 minutes. Serves 4.

German Chicken

- ~ 4 slices bacon
- ~ 1 onion, chopped
- ~ 3 cloves garlic, chopped
- ~ 1 cup sliced, cooked polish sausage
- ~ ½ cup barbeque sauce
- ~ 3 cups sauerkraut
- ~ 1 (8 oz) can tomato sauce
- ~ ¼ cup honey
- ~ 6 boneless, skinless chicken breasts
- ~ 1 tsp salt
- ~ ¼ tsp pepper

Preheat oven to 350 degrees. In small skillet, cook bacon until crisp. Drain bacon on paper towels, crumble, and set aside. Cook onion and garlic in bacon drippings, until crisp tender, about 4 minutes. In 9x13 baking dish (glass), combine sausage, sauerkraut, tomato sauce, barbeque sauce, and honey; mix well. Add cooked onion and garlic (including drippings) and stir. Sprinkle chicken breasts with salt and pepper and place on top of sauerkraut mixture. Sprinkle everything with bacon. Cover with foil and bake for 55-65 minutes or until chicken is thoroughly cooked.

Sauerkraut Pork Goulash

~ 2 tbsp vegetable oil
~ 2 medium onions, chopped
~ 1 clove garlic, chopped
~ 1 ½ tbsp paprika
~ salt and pepper
~ 2 cups chicken stock
~ 2 pounds boneless pork, cut into 1 inch cubes
~ 1 pound sauerkraut, washed and drained
~ 1 tbsp caraway seeds
~ 2 tbsp tomato puree
~ ½ cup sour cream
~ ½ cup heavy cream
~ 1 tbsp flour

Heat the oil and sauté the onions with garlic until golden. Remove from heat, stir in the paprika. Season with salt and pepper. Add ½ cup of the stock, stir, then add the pork. Arrange the sauerkraut in a layer over the pork, sprinkle with caraway seeds. Mix the tomato puree with remaining chicken stock. Add to pork mixture, bring to a boil, turn down the heat, and simmer 1 hour over very low heat, covered. Meanwhile mix sour cream and heavy cream with flour until smooth. Add to the casserole when meat is done, bring to a boil, and cook for a few minutes. Remove from heat and serve.

Bacon Baked Sauerkraut

~ 1 quart sauerkraut
~ 1 cup white sugar
~ bacon, fried and drained
~ 1 pint stewed tomatoes
~ 1 cup brown sugar

Combine tomatoes and sugar. Add sauerkraut and blend well. Bake in slow oven at 300 degrees for about 3 hours before removing from oven. Sprinkle generously with bacon bits on top.

Twice Baked Sauerkraut and Ham Potatoes

~ 6 large baking potatoes
~ ¼ cup sauerkraut juice
~ ½ cup low fat sour cream
~ ½ cup low fat mayonnaise
~ 1 cup sauerkraut, drained
~ ¼ pound boiled ham, cut in thin strips
~ ½ cup shredded cheddar cheese

Preheat oven to 375 degrees. Bake potatoes in oven for 35 minutes (or pierce with fork and microwave at medium high, turning potatoes occasionally, for 20 minutes), or until tender when fork is inserted. Remove from oven. Cut each potato in half lengthwise and scoop out center of potatoes, leaving ½ inch of potato inside skin. Mash potato insides with sauerkraut juice. Add remaining ingredients and mix well. Mound equal amounts of mixture into each potato shell, bake 10 minutes or until heated through. Serve immediately. Serves 6.

Tip: to reheat left over potatoes, bake in 350 degree oven for 10 minutes, or microwave for about 2 minutes on medium high (for one potato).

Scalloped Sauerkraut and Potatoes

~ 1 (14 oz) can sauerkraut
~ 6-8 potatoes, peeled and sliced thin
~ 1 (10 ¾ oz) can cream of mushroom soup
~ ½ cup milk

Preheat oven to 350 degrees; butter casserole dish. Pour sauerkraut in dish, and spread evenly around. Layer sliced potatoes over sauerkraut. Mix milk with mushroom soup and pour over potatoes. Bake at 350 degrees for 1 hour or until potatoes are done.

Zucchini Sauerkraut Casserole

~ 3 cups coarsely grated zucchini
~ 1 cup grated potatoes
~ ¾ cup sauerkraut, drained
~ 2 tbsp grated onions
~ 1 tbsp canola oil
~ ½ cup egg substitute
~ ¼ cup all purpose flour
~ ¾ tsp baking powder
~ 1 tsp salt
~ ⅛ tsp pepper
~ 1 cup shredded low fat cheddar cheese

Preheat oven to 350 degrees. Mix all ingredients together in a large bowl. Prepare large casserole dish with non-stick cooking spray. Pour mixture into dish; bake at 350 degrees for 1 hour. Remove from oven; sprinkle cheese over top. Bake 10-15 minutes more, or until cheese is melted and top is slightly golden. Serve.

Apple, Sauerkraut, Smokey Links Casserole

~ 1 (16 oz) can sauerkraut
~ 1 small onion, chopped
~ 1 large apple
~ 1 tbsp brown sugar
~ ½ cup cider vinegar
~ 1 (1 pound) pkg smokey links sausage

Wash, core and cut large apple into bite-sized pieces. Mix sauerkraut, onion, and apple in 1 ½ quart casserole. Season with salt and pepper to taste. Mix brown sugar and cider vinegar and pour over kraut mixture. Top with smokey link sausages; cover; bake at 350 degrees for 35 minutes.

Mashed Cauliflower and Sauerkraut Casserole

~ 1 head cauliflower, broken into flowerets
~ ½ cup mayonnaise
~ 2 garlic cloves, minced
~ salt and pepper to taste
~ ¼ tsp paprika
~ 1 cup sauerkraut, drained, rinsed, chopped
~ 2 ½ cups shredded cheddar cheese, divided
~ 1 small onion, finely chopped
~ ¼ cup bacon bits
~ 3 tbsp butter, melted

Preheat oven to 425 degrees. Lightly grease in a large casserole dish; set aside. Steam or boil cauliflower until tender; drain. In blender, whip cauliflower with the mayonnaise and garlic to a smooth consistency. (If you like it chunky, use a potato masher instead of a blender). Pour cauliflower mixture into large bowl. Add salt, pepper, paprika, sauerkraut, 1 ½ cups cheddar cheese, onion and bacon bits. Pour mixture into the prepared casserole; sprinkle with remaining 1 cup cheddar cheese and drizzle with melted butter. Bake at 425 degrees for about 10 minutes or until cheese is melted and bubbly.

Turnip and Sauerkraut Casserole

~ 1 ½ cups (12 oz) sauerkraut
~ 4 turnips, peeled and sliced
~ 1 tsp vegetable oil
~ 1 onion, chopped
~ 1 tsp caraway seed
~ 2 tsp mustard

Preheat oven to 350 degrees. Grease a deep ovenproof casserole dish. Place the turnip slices in a saucepan, cover with water, bring to a boil, and cook 10–15 minutes or until just tender. Heat the oil in a large frying pan, add the onion, and fry gently until softened. Drain the turnips well, return to the pan, add the mustard, and mix well. Place the sauerkraut and caraway seeds in the bottom of the casserole dish. Place the turnips on top of the sauerkraut in an even layer, then cover evenly with the sautéed onions. Bake uncovered for 30 minutes. Stir well before serving.

Sauerkraut Strudel

~ 1 (28 oz) can sauerkraut, drained and squeezed dry
~ 1 smoked pork chop, boned, diced
~ 1 cup shredded Swiss cheese
~ 8 sheets phyllo dough, thawed
~ ½ cup melted butter
~ ½ cup dry bread crumbs
~ sour cream

Combine sauerkraut, meat and cheese. Brush one side of dough with butter, sprinkle with 1 tablespoon bread crumbs. Top with another sheet of dough. Brush with butter; sprinkle with bread crumbs. Repeat layering with 2 more pieces of dough. Place half of the sauerkraut mixture along one short edge of dough; roll up jellyroll style. Repeat with remaining dough and sauerkraut mixture. Brush 10x15 inch jellyroll pan with butter. Bake at 400 degrees for 30 minutes or until golden brown. Cut into slices, garnish with sour cream. Serves 6.

Baked Beans with Sauerkraut

~ 1 (31 oz) can pork and beans
~ ½ pound bacon, cut up and sautéed
~ 2 onions, chopped and sautéed
~ ½ cup brown sugar
~ 1 quart sauerkraut
~ 1 pound hotdogs
~ ½ cup brown sugar

Put first 4 ingredients in baking dish and bake 2 ½ hours at 350 degrees in oven. Then add sauerkraut (drained and rinsed with cold water if it's real strong or salty), hotdogs, (cut up), and ½ cup brown sugar. Bake 30 minutes at 325 degrees.

Sauerkraut Peppers

- ~ 4 large green peppers
- ~ 2 tbsp butter
- ~ ½ pound ground pork
- ~ 3 tbsp onions, chopped
- ~ 1 cup hot rice
- ~ 1 cup sauerkraut
- ~ 2 eggs
- ~ ½ tsp salt
- ~ ⅛ tsp paprika
- ~ ¼ tsp caraway seeds

Brown pork in pan. Add onions; mix with hot cooked rice, sauerkraut, eggs, salt, paprika, and caraway seeds. Fill cleaned green peppers with mixture. Bake at 350 degrees for 45 minutes.

Sauerkraut Egg Rolls

~ 1 pound pork sausage
~ 1 medium onion, chopped
~ ½ cup chopped celery
~ ½ cup shredded carrot
~ 1 ½ cups sauerkraut
~ 2 tbsp soy sauce
~ ½ tsp sugar
~ ¼ tsp pepper
~ 1 pkg (16 oz) egg roll wrappers

Drain and rinse the sauerkraut. In large skillet, cook sausage with onion, celery, and carrots, until sausage is no longer pink and vegetables are tender crisp. In large bowl, combine sausage and vegetable mixture, sauerkraut, soy sauce, sugar, and pepper; mix well. Place ¼ cup filling in center of egg roll wrapper. Fold one corner over filling. Roll up making sure sides are tucked in as you roll. Moisten final corner with water and press edges to seal. In large saucepan, heat oil to 375 degrees. Deep fry several egg rolls for 3-4 minutes or until golden brown and crispy. Drain on paper towels. Servings: 20 egg rolls.

Sauerkraut Cabbage Roll Ups

~ 1 large head of cabbage
~ 1 pound ground beef
~ 8 fresh mushrooms, chopped
~ 1 medium onion, chopped
~ ½ green pepper, chopped
~ 2 cups cooked rice
~ 1 ½ cups sauerkraut
~ ½ tsp salt
~ ½ tsp pepper
~ 2 cups canned crushed tomatoes
~ ⅓ cup chicken broth
~ ⅛ tsp pepper
~ ¼ tsp salt
~ 1 tsp sugar
~ ½ tsp ground savory

Preheat oven to 350 degrees. Drain and rinse sauerkraut. In a large saucepan, cook cabbage covered with water for 15 minutes or until leaves are tender. Rinse in cold water. Separate 14 leaves from cabbage head and drain well.

To prepare filling: In a large fry pan, brown ground beef over medium heat until done, stirring frequently, to break up beef. Add mushrooms, onions and green peppers; cover and cook until tender. In large mixing bowl, combine meat mixture with rice, sauerkraut, salt and pepper; mix well. Divide mixture between leaves and roll up, tucking in all sides. Place two even rows seam side down in greased 9x13 inch pan.

To make sauce: In medium mixing bowl, combine crushed tomatoes, chicken broth, pepper, salt, sugar and savory. Pour over cabbage roll ups in pan. Bake uncovered for 40-45 minutes or until hot and tender. Makes 14 servings.

Frankfurter and Sauerkraut Crepes

~ 1 cup biscuit baking mix
~ 1 cup milk
~ 1 egg, slightly beaten
~ 1 stick butter
~ ½ cup onion, chopped
~ 2 tbsp vegetable oil
~ 1 (10 ¾ oz) can condensed cream of mushroom soup
~ 1 cup milk
~ 2 cups sauerkraut, drained
~ ½ pound frankfurters, thinly sliced
~ 1 tbsp chopped parsley

In bowl, combine biscuit mix, 1 cup milk, and egg; mix until blended. Heat a lightly greased 10 inch omelette pan or skillet. For each crepe, add 4 tablespoons butter, or enough to cover bottom of pan. Cook over medium heat 1 minute on each side, or until lightly browned. Lift crepes from pan using pancake turner; place wax paper. In a sauce pan, sauté onion with vegetable oil until soft. Stir in soup and milk. Measure out ½ cup sauce and set aside. Add sauerkraut, franks, and parsley to remaining sauce; mix well, cover, and heat 15 minutes. Spread sauerkraut mixture over center of each crepe, fold over sides and place in greased shallow baking dish. Pour reserved sauce over all. Bake in 350 degree oven for 15 minutes. Garnish with parsley if desired. Makes 8 crepes.

Note: If using crepe maker, follow manufacturer's instructions.

Sauerkraut and Frank Lasagna

~ 4 cups sauerkraut, drained
~ 1 pound frankfurters, thinly sliced
~ 1 (12 oz) pkg cheddar cheese, sliced
~ 9 lasagna noodles
~ 8 tbsp butter, divided
~ ½ cup onion, finely chopped
~ ½ cup parsley, finely chopped
~ 16 oz cottage cheese
~ 1 egg
~ 1 tsp caraway seed
~ 6 tbsp flour
~ 1 tsp salt
~ 1 dash cayenne pepper
~ 2 ¾ cup milk

Cook lasagna noodles according to package directions. Drain well and set aside. To prepare sauerkraut and frank filling, melt 2 tbsp butter in large skillet. Add onion and chopped parsley. Sauté over medium heat, stirring constantly, until onion is tender, about 3 minutes. Remove from heat. Stir in drained kraut, franks, cottage cheese, egg, and caraway seed. Mix until ingredients are well combined. Set aside. To prepare cheese sauce, melt remaining 6 tbsp butter in medium saucepan. Stir in flour, salt, and cayenne pepper until smooth. Cook over medium heat, stirring constantly, until mixture is smooth and bubbly. Reduce heat to low. Gradually add milk and cook, stirring constantly until mixture thickens and begins to boil. Remove from heat. Add cheese strips to sauce. Stir until cheese is melted. In ungreased 3 quart ovenproof baking dish, layer 3 noodles, ⅓ kraut and frank filling, and ½ cheese sauce. Repeat 2 times, ending with cheese sauce. Cover with foil. Bake in 375 degrees oven for 45 minutes or until center is hot and bubbly, removing foil for the last 15 minutes of baking time. For easier cutting, let stand 5 minutes after removing from oven.

Sauerkraut and Apples

~ 2 slices bacon, fried (save 2 tbsp drippings to sauté onion in)
~ 3 apples, peeled, cored, and quartered
~ pinch salt
~ 1 onion, sliced
~ 2 pounds sauerkraut
~ 1 tsp caraway seed
~ 2 raw potatoes, grated
~ brown sugar to taste

Sauté onion in drippings. Add sauerkraut. Cook 5 minutes. Add remaining ingredients and cover with soup stock or water soup stock. Best to cook slowly 30 minutes or longer if needed. Sweeten to taste with brown sugar. Very delicious.

Fried MacKraut

- ~ 2-3 tbsp butter
- ~ 3 large onions
- ~ 4 cups sauerkraut
- ~ 1 cup cooked macaroni
- ~ salt and pepper

Brown onions in butter. Add sauerkraut and cook until about half done. Add the cooked macaroni and finish frying. Add salt and pepper to taste.

Sauerkraut and Rice

~ 1 cup rice
~ 1 (32 oz) can sauerkraut, drained and rinsed
~ 4 tbsp oil
~ ½ cup diced onions
~ paprika, salt, pepper, and garlic to taste

Cook rice and drain. Fry onion in oil. Add seasonings, kraut, and fry with onions about 20 minutes. In baking dish, layer kraut mixture and rice. Bake at 300 degrees for 30 minutes. Very good served with pork chops.

Glorified Sauerkraut

~ 1 (27 oz) can sauerkraut
~ 1 (4 oz) can mushrooms
~ 3 tbsp butter
~ 1 (28 oz) can tomatoes, diced
~ 3 onions, chopped
~ 1 green pepper, chopped
~ ¼ cup sugar (heaping)

Drain sauerkraut and mushrooms; do not rinse kraut. Sauté onions in butter. Add green pepper and mushrooms. Cook a while longer then combine all ingredients in buttered casserole dish. Mix well. Bake with cover at 350 degrees for 1 hour, then ½ hour uncovered.

Steamed Spice Sauerkraut

~ 2 pounds sauerkraut
~ 1 tbsp cooking oil
~ ½ cup finely chopped onions
~ 1 tbsp sugar
~ 2 cups cold water
~ 5 whole juniper berries, 6 whole black peppercorns, 2 small bay leaves, ¼ tsp caraway seeds, and 1 whole allspice, wrapped together in cheesecloth
~ ½ pound boneless smoked pork loin
~ ½ pound Canadian style bacon in 1 piece
~ 1 large raw potato, peeled

Drain the sauerkraut, wash it thoroughly under cold running water (in colander), and let it soak in a pot of cold water for 10-20 minutes, depending upon its acidity. A handful at a time, squeeze the sauerkraut vigorously until it is completely dry. In a heavy 3-4 quart casserole dish, put the 1 tablespoon of cooking oil in over low heat. Add the chopped onions and cook, stirring frequently, for 8-10 minutes, or until the onions are light brown. Add the sauerkraut, sugar and 2 cups of water, and mix together thoroughly, separating the strands of sauerkraut with a fork. Bury the bag of spices in the sauerkraut and place the pork and bacon on top of it. Bring to a boil over high heat, then reduce the heat to lowest point; cover the casserole and cook, undisturbed for 20 minutes. Grate the raw potato directly into the casserole; with a fork stir it into the sauerkraut mixture. Cover the casserole tightly, and cook over low heat for 1 ½ - 2 hours, or until the sauerkraut has absorbed most of its cooking liquid and the meat is tender when pierced with tip of a fork. Remove and discard the spices. Taste for seasoning.

To serve, cut the meat into ¼ inch slices. Then transfer the sauerkraut to a large heated platter. Spread the sauerkraut into an even mound and arrange the slices of meat on top.

Stewed Kraut

~ 2 (15 oz) cans of sauerkraut
~ 2 (15 oz) cans of stewed tomatoes
~ ¼ cup brown sugar

Preheat oven to 350 degrees. Mix all ingredients in a bowl. Pour into casserole dish and cook for 1 hour at 350 degrees. Serve. Great with roast pork, grilled pork, or sausage.

Cola Sauerkraut

~ ½ cup butter
~ 2 medium onions, chopped
~ 2 (16 oz) jars sauerkraut
~ 1 (12 oz) can cola flavoured carbonated beverage
~ ½ cup water (optional)

Melt the butter in a large skillet or Dutch oven over medium heat. Sauté onions in butter until translucent. Stir in sauerkraut and cola. Cover, reduce heat to low, and simmer for 1 hour, adding up to ½ cup of water if necessary to prevent sticking. Remove cover and put heat to medium for at least 15 minutes, or until sauerkraut glistens. Serve. Goes great with pork!

Sauerkraut Delight

~ 1 (32 oz) can sauerkraut
~ 1 (28 oz) can diced tomatoes
~ 1 pkg all-beef wieners
~ ½ pound cheddar cheese

Place layer sauerkraut in 2 quart casserole bowl; then layer of wieners (cut in half), layer of tomatoes (no juice), layer of cheese. Repeat layering to top. Place in preheated 400 degree oven for 45 minutes.

Mother-in-law Sauerkraut

~ 4 slices turkey bacon, sliced
~ 1 (16 oz) can sauerkraut
~ 1 head cabbage, chopped
~ 1 large onion
~ 1 tbsp butter
~ ½ tsp salt
~ ⅛ tsp pepper

In a small skillet, cook bacon until crisp. Combine remaining ingredients into slow cooker. Pour bacon over all. Cook, covered on low heat for 3-5 hours. Serves 8.

Whitefish and Sauerkraut

~ 2 pounds whitefish fillets (or perch, cod or trout)
~ 1 cup red onions, finely chopped
~ ⅓ cup butter
~ 1 (28 oz) can sauerkraut, drained
~ 1 cup chicken bouillon
~ 1 medium red onion thinly sliced in rings

Cut fillets in serving size portions. Sauté onions in 2 tablespoons butter until translucent. Add sauerkraut and bouillon. Simmer about 30 minutes. Meanwhile, dust fillets with flour and fry in remaining butter 3-4 minutes on each side or until fish is opaque and flakes easily. Arrange in serving dish and keep warm. In the same pan, sauté onion rings. Spread sauerkraut over fillets and garnish with onion rings. Serves 6.

Orange Roughly with Orange Sauerkraut

~ 2 cups (16 oz) sauerkraut
~ 1 cup orange juice
~ 6 (2 pounds) orange roughy fillets
~ 1 stick unsalted butter, cold and cut into pieces
~ 1 orange, sliced (for garnish)

Drain the sauerkraut and combine ¼ cup of the liquid with the orange juice in a large skillet. Reserve sauerkraut. Bring this liquid to a simmer and add the roughy fillets. Poach about 2-3 minutes or until the flesh can be flaked with a fork. Transfer the cooked fillets to a platter and keep warm. Pour ½ cup of the liquid into a saucepan, bring to a simmer, and reduce to ¼ cup. Add the sauerkraut to the skillet and simmer until the remaining liquid is absorbed and the sauerkraut is hot. Meanwhile, whisk the cold pieces of butter into the reduced, simmering liquid to make an orange-flavored French butter sauce. Do not boil the sauce; remove it from heat as soon as the butter is melted. Place a small mound of sauerkraut in center of each plate and place fillet on top. Spoon a little sauce around the food and garnish with an orange slice. Serves 6.

Duck and Sauerkraut

~ 1 (3 pound) duck
~ 2 quarts sauerkraut
~ 2 small yellow onions, peeled
~ 3 tbsp brown sugar
~ pepper to taste

Place the duck in a roasting pan and roast in a 400 degree oven until lightly browned, about 25 minutes. Remove and cool a bit. Disregard the fat in a pan. Place the duck in a very close fitting casserole and pack the sauerkraut around and under the duck. Put the remaining kraut along with the juice, on top. Add the onions to the pot. Add 1 cup water and top with brown sugar and pepper. Cover and bake at 325 degrees until the duck is very tender, about 1 ½ hours. It is traditional to serve this dish with a green salad and mashed potatoes.

Braised Pheasant with Sauerkraut

- ~ 1 pheasant, singed and cleaned
- ~ 2 pounds sauerkraut
- ~ 2 cups broth
- ~ 8 crushed juniper berries
- ~ 4 tbsp butter
- ~ 3 tbsp oil
- ~ 1 tsp salt
- ~ 1 tsp fresh ground pepper

Combine the sauerkraut with the broth and juniper berries; simmer one hour, covered in a large braising pan or Dutch oven. Heat the fat in a heavy skillet and brown the pheasant on all sides over fairly high heat (if you want to cook 2 birds, it is wiser to brown one at a time). When they are nicely browned, salt and pepper them and place in the braising pan on the sauerkraut. Cover and bake in a 375 degree oven 45 minutes or until pheasant is tender. Pheasant is done when internal temperature is 160-165 degrees measured in the thickest part of the thigh without touching the bone. Letting the pheasant rest 12-15 minutes can increase the internal temperature as much as 10 degrees. Arrange on a platter with the sauerkraut and serve with fried hominy or potatoes. Serves 2.

Sauerkraut Moose Balls

~ 1 pound ground moose
~ ½ pound ground pork
~ 3 eggs
~ 1 cup sauerkraut, squeezed dry and finely chopped
~ ½ cup processed cheese spread
~ 1 small onion, minced
~ 1 tsp minced garlic
~ salt and pepper
~ 1 cup diced fine bread crumbs
~ oil for deep frying

Mix together all ingredients, except bread crumbs. Roll into 1 inch balls, then in bread crumbs. Place on cookie sheet and chill for 30 minutes. Heat oil to 400 degrees and deep fry balls a few at a time for about 30 seconds or until golden brown. Drain on paper towels. Serve with hot mustard.

Desserts

Chocolate Sauerkraut Cake

~ ¾ cup sauerkraut, drained and chopped
~ 1 ½ cups sugar
~ ½ cup butter
~ 3 eggs
~ 1 tsp pure vanilla
~ 2 cups all purpose flour
~ 1 tsp baking powder
~ 1 tsp baking soda
~ ½ tsp salt
~ 1 cup water
~ ½ cup unsweetened cocoa powder

Preheat oven 350°F. Sift all dry ingredients together. Cream sugar, butter, and vanilla. Beat eggs in one at a time. Add dry ingredients to creamed mixture alternatively with water. Add sauerkraut; mix thoroughly. Pour into greased cake pan or pans. Bake 30-40 minutes until cake tests done. Frost.

Cream Cheese Frosting for Chocolate Sauerkraut Cake

~ 1 (3 oz) pkg cream cheese
~ 6 tbsp butter
~ 1 tsp vanilla
~ 2 cups powdered sugar
~ 1 tbsp milk

Soften cream cheese and butter. Combine all ingredients and beat until smooth. To make frosting spread easily, add more milk, if necessary.

Chocolate Sauerkraut Cupcakes

Follow the chocolate sauerkraut cake recipe completely, except you pour mixture into a cupcake pan (muffin pan) and bake until cupcakes are done.

Note: Cupcakes usually require less baking time then cake. Check regularly.

Sauerkraut Apple Cake

- ~ 2 cups all purpose flour
- ~ 2 tsp baking powder
- ~ 2 tsp ground cinnamon
- ~ 1 tsp baking soda
- ~ 1 tsp salt
- ~ ½ tsp grated nutmeg
- ~ 1 cup sugar
- ~ ½ cup light brown sugar, packed
- ~ 4 eggs
- ~ 1 (16 oz) can sauerkraut, rinsed and thoroughly drained
- ~ 1 apple, peeled, cored, and finely chopped (yellow delicious apple)
- ~ 1 cup coarsely chopped walnuts or pecans

Frosting:
- ~ 1 (8 oz) pkg cream cheese at room temperature
- ~ ½ cup (1 stick) butter at room temperature
- ~ 1 pound confectioners sugar
- ~ 1 tsp vanilla extract
- ~ 2 tsps ground cinnamon
- ~ 1 tbsp grated orange zest
- ~ ⅛ tsp salt

Preheat oven to 325 degrees. In a large mixing bowl, whisk together flour, baking powder, cinnamon, baking soda, salt and nutmeg; set aside. In another large mixing bowl, combine the sugars and whisk in the eggs, and then the oil; blend well. Stir in the drained sauerkraut, apples and nuts. Add the dry ingredients and stir until moistened. Pour into a 9x13 inch glass baking dish; bake for 35 minutes, or until the top of the cake springs back when touched with your finger and the cake is just beginning to pull away from the sides of the dish. Cool the cake completely before frosting.

Prepare the frosting: In a large mixing bowl, beat the cream cheese and butter until blended. Gradually add the confectioners sugar, then the vanilla, cinnamon, orange zest and salt; beat well. Spread on the cooled cake. Keep the cake refrigerated until serving time or the frosting becomes too soft.

Note: Because of the cream cheese in the frosting, the cake should be refrigerated, but the flavor will be better if you bring it to room temperature before serving. Serves 12.

Sauerkraut Cream Pie

~ ½ cup sauerkraut, drained, rinsed
~ 2 cups sugar
~ 1 cup milk
~ 2 tbsp yellow corn meal
~ 2 tbsp lemon juice
~ ½ cup butter
~ 3 tbsp flour
~ 5 eggs, well beaten
~ 1 tsp vanilla

Drain the kraut and rinse with cold water. Squeeze dry. Cream butter, sugar and add flour, cornmeal, eggs, milk, vanilla, and lemon juice. Add to drained kraut. Beat well and pour into two unbaked 9" pie crusts. Bake 55-60 minutes or until knife inserted comes out clean.

Sauerkraut Custard Pie

~ 1 crust for a 9" pie, unbaked
~ 2 ½ cups milk
~ ¾ cup sauerkraut, drained, rinsed, chopped
~ ½ cup sugar
~ 3 eggs
~ 1 tsp vanilla extract
~ ¼ tsp salt

Preheat oven to 425 degrees. In a large bowl, combine milk, eggs, sauerkraut, sugar, vanilla, and salt. Pour mixture into pie shell. Bake at 425 degrees for 35 minutes or until knife inserted 1" from the edge comes out clean. Enjoy!

Coconut Crunch Surprise Bars

Crust:
- ~ 1 pkg (18.25 oz) German chocolate cake mix
- ~ ½ cup crushed pretzels
- ~ ½ cup butter, melted
- ~ 1 egg

Filling:
- ~ ¼ cup sugar
- ~ 1 cup dark corn syrup
- ~ 2 eggs
- ~ ¾ cup pecans, chopped
- ~ 1 cup butterscotch chips
- ~ 1 cup coconut
- ~ 1 ¼ cup sauerkraut, rinsed and drained
- ~ 1 cup semisweet chocolate chips

Preheat oven to 350 degrees. In large bowl combine all crust ingredients; mix at low speed until blended. Press into bottom of greased 9x13 inch pan. Bake 15 minutes or until crust puffs up and appears dry; cool 5 minutes. In large bowl, combine sugar, corn syrup, and eggs; mix at low speed until well blended. Stir in remaining ingredients. Spoon evenly over partially baked crust. Bake an additional 30-40 minutes or until golden brown. Cool 10 minutes, then run a knife around sides of pan to loosen. Cool an additional hour and cut into bars.

Coconut Sauerkraut Macaroon Cookies

~ 1 pkg dry sugar cookie mix
~ 2 egg whites
~ 1 tsp almond extract
~ 1 cup sauerkraut, drained and rinsed
~ ¾ cup flaked coconut
~ ½ cup melted semisweet chocolate

Preheat oven to 375 degrees. Combine cookie mix, 1 egg white, almond extract, and sauerkraut. Stir until thoroughly blended. Shape dough into one inch balls and dip into remaining egg white, slightly beaten. Roll in coconut and place in ungreased cookie sheet (line cookie sheet with parchment paper before placing the cookie balls on it). Bake at 375 degrees for 8 minutes on baking sheet. Remove to cooling rack. Once cooled, drizzle melted chocolate over to decorate.

Sauerkraut Cookies

~ 1 stick butter, softened
~ 1 cup sugar
~ 1 egg
~ 1 cup sauerkraut, well drained and chopped
~ 1 tsp vanilla extract
~ 1 ½ cups flour
~ ⅓ cup Hershey's unsweetened baking cocoa
~ 1 tsp baking powder
~ ½ tsp baking soda
~ ¼ tsp salt

Cream butter and sugar together. Add egg and blend well. Stir in sauerkraut and vanilla extract. Sift flour, cocoa, baking powder, baking soda, and salt together. Stir into creamed mixture. Drop by teaspoonfuls on greased cookie sheet. Bake at 350 degrees for 10 minutes. Makes 12 cookies.

Sauerkraut Brownies

~ ¾ cup salted butter
~ 1 ½ cups sugar
~ 3 eggs
~ 1 tsp almond extract
~ ½ cup + 2 tbsp flour
~ ½ cup + 2 tbsp unsweetened cocoa powder
~ 1 pound sauerkraut, drained and rinsed
~ 1 cup water (approximate)
~ ½ cup whole pecans
~ ½ cup butterscotch chips

Preheat oven to 350 degrees. Line a 9x9 baking pan with foil and spray with cooking spray. In a medium saucepan, melt butter over medium heat. Stir in sugar until blended, about 2 minutes. Remove from heat and beat in eggs 1 at a time; mixing well after each addition. Stir in almond extract. In a medium bowl, sift the flour and cocoa together. Add the flour mixture to the butter mixture, stirring until combined. In a blender, puree sauerkraut with approximately 1 cup water. Drain, then squeeze the sauerkraut until water is removed. Mix sauerkraut into batter. Stir in butterscotch chips and pecans. Spread mixture in prepared pan. Bake 45-50 minutes.

Tip: You may substitute walnuts or almonds for pecans. You may also substitute chocolate, white chocolate, or peanut butter instead of butterscotch chips.

Lemon Kraut Ice Cream

- ~ 2 tbsp cornstarch
- ~ 1 cup sugar
- ~ ¼ cup grated lemon peel (about 6 lemons)
- ~ 1 ½ cups milk
- ~ 2 eggs, separated
- ~ ½ cup each: lemon juice, sauerkraut juice
- ~ 1 quart heavy cream, whipped

Mix cornstarch, sugar and lemon peel in saucepan. Stir in milk. Cook over medium heat, stirring constantly, until mixture thickens and boils 1 minute. Remove from heat. Beat egg yolks in large bowl. Gradually blend in milk mixture. Cool. Stir in lemon juice and kraut juice. Beat egg whites until stiff but not dry. Fold with cream into cornstarch mixture. Turn into refrigerator trays. Freeze until ice crystals form around edges of trays. Turn mixture into large bowl and beat well. Return to trays. Freeze until firm. Mellow in refrigerator for ½ hour before serving. Makes 2 quarts.

Sauerkraut Candy

~ 1 ¼ cups cocoa powder
~ 1 cup evaporated milk
~ 1 cup sauerkraut, drained, chopped
~ 12 ounces semisweet chocolate
~ 4 cups sugar
~ 1 tsp vanilla
~ 10 ounces miniature marshmallows

Boil sugar, cocoa, and evaporated milk to soft boil stage (234 degrees). Add chocolate chips and vanilla. Stir until chips are melted. Beat in marshmallows and kraut. Kraut must be well rinsed and drained — almost dry. Beat until thoroughly combined and pour into buttered pan to set. Cool and cut into squares. 18 servings.

Sauerkraut Haystacks

~ ½ cup sauerkraut, drained
~ 1 bag (10 oz) chocolate chips
~ ⅛ tsp cinnamon
~ ¼ cup chow mein noodles
~ ½ cup almonds, toasted

In a double boiler, melt chocolate chips. Add cinnamon and mix to combine. Add drained sauerkraut, chow mein noodles, and toasted almonds. Mix well to coat everything with chocolate. Line a sheet pan with wax paper and drop teaspoonfuls of haystacks onto it. Put into the refrigerator until cool and hardened, about 15-20 minutes. Makes about 18-24 haystacks, depending on how big your teaspoons are.

Miscellaneous

German Sauerkraut Dip

~ 1 (8 oz) pkg cream cheese, softened
~ 2 tbsp grated onion
~ 1 tbsp catsup
~ 1 (4 oz) can sauerkraut, undrained

Combine all ingredients in blender or processor until well blended. Add milk if mixture is too thick. Serve with pretzels.

Sauerkraut Crab Dip

- ~ 1 (8 oz) pkg cream cheese, softened
- ~ ¼ cup sour cream
- ~ 1 ½ cups sauerkraut, drained
- ~ 1 (6 oz) can crab meat, drained
- ~ ¼ cup chopped parsley
- ~ salt and pepper to taste
- ~ pretzels

In a mixing bowl beat cream cheese and sour cream until well blended. Stir in remaining ingredients except pretzels. Serve with pretzels. Serves 12.

German Sauerkraut Relish

~ 1 (15 oz) can sauerkraut, drained
~ ½ cup green pepper, chopped
~ ½ cup onions, chopped
~ ½ cup celery, chopped
~ 1 medium sized cucumber, diced
~ 1 (4 oz) jar pimento
~ ¼ cup salad oil
~ ½ cup apple cider vinegar
~ 1 cup sugar

Put all ingredients together; place in covered container. Let stand overnight in the refrigerator. Ready to serve.

Kraut Pineapple Relish

~ 2 cups drained sauerkraut
~ ½ cup crushed pineapple

Stir sauerkraut and pineapple together in a microwavable bowl. Cover and microwave on high for 3-4 minutes or until warmed through. Serve over grilled pork or poultry.

Frankfurters with Hot Kraut Relish

~ 1 medium sized green pepper, diced
~ 2 cups sauerkraut, undrained (16 oz)
~ ½ cup water
~ 1 tbsp Worcestershire sauce
~ ¾ cup grated carrot (1 medium carrot)
~ 6 frankfurters

In saucepan, combine green pepper, undrained kraut, water, and Worcestershire sauce. Cover over medium heat, stirring occasionally, 5-10 minutes or until green pepper is tender. Add carrot.

Meanwhile, broil frankfurters 3-4 inches from source of heat on each side or until frankfurters are brown. Drain kraut relish, if necessary. Serve relish with frankfurters. Serves 6.

Sauerkraut Onion Topping

~ 2 tbsp oil
~ 1 large mild onion, peeled and sliced
~ 1 small green pepper, sliced
~ 1 small red pepper, sliced
~ 1 can (16 oz) sauerkraut, drained

Sauté onion and peppers in oil until tender, but not browned. Add drained sauerkraut and a few tablespoons of water. Heat through. Use as a topping for hotdogs or knockwurst. Serves 6.

Sauerkraut Balls

~ 3 cups sauerkraut, drained
~ 1 medium onion, finely chopped
~ 1 cup cooked ham, finely chopped
~ ½ medium garlic clove, crushed
~ 6 tbsp flour
~ ⅛ tsp seasoned salt
~ 1 tbsp parsley
~ 2 eggs
~ fine cracker meal
~ 3 tbsp butter
~ 1 cup cooked corned beef, finely chopped
~ 1 egg
~ 1 tsp Worcestershire sauce
~ ½ cup beef bouillon
~ 2 tbsp water

Melt butter; add onion and garlic; cook over low heat for 5 minutes. Stir in ham, corned beef, and flour; cook until brown. Combine eggs, sauerkraut, seasoned salt, Worcestershire sauce, parsley, and beef stock. Cook over low heat, stirring occasionally, until thickened. Remove from heat and chill. Shape into walnut-sized balls. Beat remaining eggs with water; coat balls with mixture; roll in cracker meal. Deep-fry at 375 degrees for 2-3 minutes or until brown. Drain on paper towel. Serve warm.

Note: Sauerkraut balls may be frozen on a cookie sheet and then placed in a bag. Simply thaw before deep frying.

Beef Kraut Balls

- ~ 14 rye crisp crackers
- ~ 3 cups sauerkraut, drained lightly (see note)
- ~ 1 (12 oz) can corned beef
- ~ 1 egg, slightly beaten
- ~ 1 tbsp sugar
- ~ 1 cup all purpose flour
- ~ 5 cups peanut oil (for deep frying)

In food processor bowl, process the crackers until finely ground. Set aside. To the processor bowl, add the sauerkraut and corned beef; process until well combined. Add the egg, sugar, flour, and cracker crumbs; process again until just mixed. Using a 1 inch cookie scoop or a tablespoon, shape the mixture into 1 inch balls; set aside. Meanwhile, in a deep fryer, heat the oil to 375 degrees. Place a few balls at a time in the hot oil and fry for about 1 minute, or until browned. Remove with a slotted spoon; drain on paper towel. Repeat until all balls are fried. These fried balls may be frozen, then thawed and reheated at 400 degrees in oven for 15 minutes.

Note: the sauerkraut should have some juice still included for flavor, but the mixture should not be soppy.

Sauerkraut Cheeseball

~   1 (16 oz) can sauerkraut, drained
~   1 ½ pound grated cheddar cheese
~   ½ cup onion, chopped
~   ½ cup green pepper, chopped
~   2 hard cooked eggs, chopped
~   ½ cup soda crackers
~   1 tbsp sugar
~   ¼ - ½ cup mayonnaise
~   1 cup walnuts, chopped

Mix sauerkraut, cheese, onion, green pepper, eggs, crackers, and sugar. Add mayonnaise to moisten. Shape into ball and sprinkle or roll into chopped walnuts. Refrigerate and serve with crackers. Makes 2 large balls.

Sauerkraut on Toast

~ 4 slices whole grain bread
~ 1 tbsp sesame butter (usually purchased at oriental store)
~ 1 cup sauerkraut

Toast bread; then spread with sesame butter. Grill for 1 minute. Place sauerkraut in pan and simmer for 2 minutes. Spread on grilled bread. Serves 4.

Pigs in Blankets

~ 1 pkg (14 oz) store bought puff pastry, thawed
~ 50 cocktail hotdogs
~ 2 large eggs, lightly beaten with 1 tbsp water for egg wash
~ ½ cup sauerkraut, drained

Preheat oven to 425 degrees. Cut pastry into ¾ by 3 inch strips, wrap around hotdogs, sealing with a dab of water. Brush egg wash over pastry. Bake until golden brown, 5-8 minutes. Top with sauerkraut. Serve.

Salsa Ole

~ 1 can (15 oz) black beans, drained and rinsed
~ ½ cup packed sauerkraut
~ ⅓ cup fresh cilantro, chopped
~ 1 can (4 oz) green chilis, chopped
~ 2 tbsp lime juice
~ 2 large tomatoes, seeded and chopped
~ ¼ cup green onions, finely chopped
~ 1 red pepper, chopped
~ 1 yellow pepper, chopped
~ 1 green pepper, chopped
~ 1 red onion, chopped (large)
~ tortilla chips

Drain, rinse, and chop sauerkraut. In medium bowl, combine all ingredients, stirring well. Cover and refrigerate at least 2 hours before serving. Serve with tortilla chips. Makes about 3 cups or 10 servings.

Substitution: you may substitute the 2 large tomatoes for 1 large can (28 oz) crushed tomatoes, if you desire.

Pineapple Sauerkraut

~ 2 pounds fresh sauerkraut
~ 5 cups unsweetened pineapple juice (2-20 oz cans)
~ A 1 ½ - 2 pound ripe pineapple

Drain the sauerkraut, wash it thoroughly under cold running water; let it soak in a pot of cold water for 10-20 minutes, depending on its acidity. A handful at a time, squeeze the sauerkraut until it is completely dry. Combine the sauerkraut and pineapple juice in a heavy 3-4 quart saucepan, and bring to a boil over high heat, stirring with a fork to separate the sauerkraut strands. Reduce the heat to its lowest point and cover the pan tightly. Simmer, undisturbed, for 1 ½ - 2 hours or until the sauerkraut has absorbed most of its cooking liquid. With a long, sharp knife, cut the top 1 ½ inches off the pineapple. Set the top aside. Hollow out the pineapple carefully, leaving a ⅛ - ¼ inch layer of the fruit in the shell. Remove and discard the woody core of the hollowed out fruit and cut the fruit into ½ inch cubes. Stir the diced pineapple into the cooked sauerkraut, cook for a minute or two; then pour the entire mixture into a large sieve set over a bowl. When all the liquid has drained through, pile the sauerkraut into the pineapple shell. Cover with the reserved pineapple top and serve on a large plate. If you like, any remaining sauerkraut may be presented mounded on the plate around the pineapple. Pineapple sauerkraut is traditionally served with roasted smoked pork.

Baked Potato Topping

~ ¼ cup sour cream
~ ¼ cup sauerkraut
~ ½ tsp dill weed
~ 1-2 tsp crumbled bacon

Combine all ingredients except bacon. Place a heaping teaspoon (or as desired), of mixture on baked potato halves; sprinkle with bacon.

Sauerkraut Burrito

~ Wrapper (flour tortilla or other wrap)
~ 2 layers cheddar cheese
~ 1 layer chopped green peppers
~ 1 layer chopped tomatoes
~ 1 layer salsa
~ 2 layers cooked pinto beans (or refried beans)
~ 2 layers sauerkraut

Wrap the ingredients and cook them at 350 degrees for 30 minutes. Enjoy!

Sausage Sauerkraut Pizza

~ 2 (8 oz) pkgs crescent rolls
~ 3 tbsp olive oil
~ 1 pound sausage with sage
~ 2 (8 oz) pkgs cream cheese, softened
~ 1 cup mayonnaise
~ 1 (16 oz) pkg dried ranch salad dressing mix
~ ½ cup chopped onion
~ 1 cup sauerkraut, well drained
~ 8 ounces cheddar cheese, grated

Preheat oven to 350 degrees. Unroll crescent rolls, but do not separate the rolls; press them into a jelly-roll or pizza pan. Bake for 10 minutes until dough is golden brown. Set aside to cool. Brown sausage and onion in olive oil until sausage is brown and done. Remove from heat. Drain well. Set aside. Mix cream cheese, mayonnaise and salad dressing mix in a bowl and spread over the cooled crust. Top with sausage and onion mixture. Layer all of sauerkraut over top sausage and onion mixture. Sprinkle cheddar cheese over all. Cut and serve.

Reuben Cheesecake

~ 1 ½ cups rye cracker crumbs
~ ¼ cup plus 2 tbsp melted butter
~ 2 (8 oz) pkgs cream cheese, softened
~ ¼ cup flour
~ 1 (8 oz) bottle Thousand Island dressing
~ 1 (8 oz) can sauerkraut, well drained
~ 1 (12 oz) can corned beef, well broken up
~ 4 eggs

Preheat oven to 300 degrees. Put crumbs and butter in a 9 inch spring form pan. Mix well and press into place. Whip cream cheese until fluffy. Add eggs, beat well. Add remaining ingredients. Mix until well blended. Pour into prepared pan. Bake at 300 degrees for 1 hour. Cool. Cover and chill to serve.

Reuben Omelette

- ~ 8 large eggs
- ~ 1 tsp caraway seed
- ~ 1 cup sauerkraut, drained
- ~ 4 tbsp butter
- ~ 8 Swiss cheese slices, thin
- ~ ¾ pounds corned beef brisket, thinly sliced
- ~ 4 tbsp Thousand Island dressing
- ~ 5 Gherkins

Have corned beef sliced into slices, about 12 pieces if possible. Drain sauerkraut through strainer over bowl until very well drained. Discard liquid. Mince 1 gherkin and add to Thousand Island dressing. Break eggs into a medium bowl and ½ cup water and caraway seeds. Beat eggs until thoroughly blended. Place omelette pan over medium heat. When hot, add 1 tablespoon solid butter to pan. Tilt to coat sides and bottom. Turn heat to medium high. Pour in one quarter of eggs. Use wide spatula or fork, pull cooked eggs toward center, allowing uncooked part to flow to outside. While top is still moist and creamy, add 2 slices Swiss cheese to one of omelette, top with ¼ of the corned beef, then top with ¼ cup sauerkraut. Fold the other side over and immediately remove to serving plate. Keep in barely warm oven, while preparing remaining 3 omelettes. Wipe pan with paper towels between each omelette. To serve, top each omelette with ¼ of the dressing and serve 1 gherkin along side of the omelette. Serves 4.

Substitution: You may substitute corned beef for either smoked turkey slices or pastrami slices for a different taste.

Hash Brown Reuben

~ ¾ cup hash brown potatoes
~ ¾ cup cooked corned beef, sliced thin and heated
~ 1 cup sauerkraut, drained and rinsed
~ 1 cup Swiss cheese, sliced thin
~ 1 cup Thousand Island dressing

Grill hash browns as directed. Transfer to serving plate and top with corned beef, sauerkraut, and Swiss cheese. Broil (or microwave) until hot and bubbly.

Cheddar and Poppy Seed Scones

~ 1 ¾ cups all purpose flour
~ 2 tbsp poppy seeds
~ 2 tbsp sugar
~ 1 tsp baking powder
~ ½ tsp baking soda
~ ½ tsp salt
~ 6 tbsp butter
~ 1 egg
~ 1 cup sauerkraut, drained, squeezed dry, and chopped
~ 1 cup medium sharp cheddar cheese
~ ¾ cup sour cream
~ ⅓ cup thinly sliced green onions

Preheat oven to 400 degrees. Grease large baking sheet. In large bowl, stir together flour, poppy seeds, sugar, baking powder, baking soda, and salt. Cut in butter, using pastry blender or 2 knives until mixture resembles coarse crumbs. In a small bowl, stir together egg, sauerkraut, cheese, sour cream and onion. Add to dry ingredients. Stir until combined. Transfer dough to lightly floured surface. Pat into an eight by eight inch square. Cut dough into four four-inch squares. Cut each piece diagonally in half to make eight triangles. Place scones one inch apart on prepared baking sheet. Bake 16-20 minutes or until golden brown. Serve warm.

Sauerkraut Smoothie

~   1 cup Red Punch
~   2 cups vanilla ice cream
~   1 cup ice cubes
~   1 cup sauerkraut
~   1 ½ cups vanilla yogurt
~   1 cup fruit (any type)

Put all ingredients in a blender. Blend until fairly thin. Chill in freezer for about 5-10 minutes. Serve in cups. Garnish with lemons or limes.

Sauerkraut Juice Cocktail

~ 2 cups sauerkraut juice
~ 2 tbsp lemon juice
~ ¼ tsp caraway seeds
~ ½ cup fresh apples, finely diced

Combine ingredients in order listed. Serve cold in cocktail glasses.

Conclusion

HAVE YOU EVER wondered what happened to all those good ol' recipes grandma used to cook? You may have spent needless hours trying to search out and locate some of her sauerkraut recipes, only to end up frustrated with no hope of acquiring them. Due to present day fast food cooking styles, 'grandma's old-time, home-style cooking' is quickly becoming a lost art for both modern day and future generations. In my willingness to devote much time and research, I did all the hard work of gathering all types of recipes involving sauerkraut and placing them all into one book for your convenience.

So for all you sauerkraut lovers that cannot seem to find that special sauerkraut recipe, nor the time to search it out, this book is for you. I'm sure many of you will be amazed at all the different variations and dishes that use sauerkraut. I know I was surprised. So now when you have a taste for sauerkraut, just pick up the "Sauerkraut's Incredible Fascinations" cookbook, look it up, cook it, and eat it up! Many people, including myself, have cooked, tasted, and enjoyed these delicious recipes. I believe you, your families and friends will all get the delightful satisfaction and enjoyment with each recipe as all previous cooks (and grandmas) have.

It is my greatest pleasure to share with each one of you the many sauerkraut recipes from all over the world, that have been handed down through the ages. I'm sure your guests will be highly impressed by the meals and dishes you have prepared for them from this book.

It is my desire that this book will help re-establish home style cooking into homes worldwide, so future generations will not lose the art, nor the taste, that only home style cooking gives, especially with sauerkraut. As grandmas of old know, both sauerkraut and home style cooking go hand-in-hand. May this book serve as an encouragement to all generations to incorporate home style cooking with sauerkraut along side fast food and convenient styles of living and eating.

Finally, I want to extend my heartfelt thanks and appreciation to each one of you for purchasing "Sauerkraut's Incredible Fascinations." Because of your purchase, many lives and appetites will enjoy ultimate delight in savoring the goodness and taste of sauerkraut, especially yours! For special dinners, I believe your guests will find these recipes quite delicious and fulfilling at any table. It is both a great pleasure and blessing to have the opportunity to share these delicious sauerkraut recipes with you, your family, and your friends.

Lightning Source UK Ltd.
Milton Keynes UK
UKHW021252260721
387785UK00006B/474